SHTARKER
The Legend of Dan Tabas

[shtark-*er*]
—noun
1. a strong-minded person, a mover and shaker.

Peter Davidson
with Susan Tabas Tepper & Louis La Palombara III

Table of Contents

Dedication 4

Foreword 5

Preface 7

Early Years 8

Mr. Downingtown 28

A Pasture Becomes A Goldmine 44

The Loan Ranger 80

Family First 92

A Prolific Giver 108

Patron of the Arts
Collector of Classics 120

One Of A Kind 128

Postscript 148

Dedication

In loving memory of Dan Tabas

*Large streams from little fountains flow,
Tall oaks from little acorns grow*
English proverb

Dedicated to our grandchildren

**Adam Todd Stempel
Alexander Cody Stempel
Baron Oldrich Fercos Tabas Hantig
Brittany Morgan Wurzak
Chelsea Arielle Wurzak
Chet Adam Stofman
Dagny Kent Tabas Tepper
Elizabeth Rebecca Tabas Carson
Fitz Daniel Tabas Tepper
Gregory Rome Stofman
Jake Michael Wurzak
Jason Bryan Tabas
Jessica Erin Stempel
Lily Ashley Stofman
Major Corl Tabas Tepper
Maxwell Hunter Stofman
Melissa Tamara Tabas
Samuel Bradford Tabas
Stephanie Pearl Tabas
Theodore Hershel Tabas**

*with love,
Grandma Evelyn Rome Tabas*

Foreword

Knowing someone like Dan Tabas can definitely be life enhancing, and I'm sure that sentiment is shared with many others who had the good fortune to know him. I had a copy of his father's book, *Mulke,* in my office and I can remember Dan mentioning he'd like to do something similar someday. I'm happy to know Susan worked with him on creating this biography – he'd be very proud.

Dan's story is an inspiring one, as was his father's, and it's also a great romance. Evelyn was and remained the love of his life, and Evelyn's devotion was equal to his. To see the legacy they've created is in great evidence in Susan's book, as is their magnanimous approach to life. It is truly a great family and their contribution to society is to be admired.

I'd like to thank Susan for putting this book together. It is clearly a labor of love and is of great value to Dan's family and friends.

I am proud to have known Dan Tabas, and this book is a wonderful tribute to a very special man.

Donald J. Trump

Dan and Evelyn Tabas

> *When I think back over what the Tabas family has meant to the city of Philadelphia in the last fifty years, the things you've done, the development you've created, the jobs you have put into place for people to hold and earn great livings, the charitable contributions that the two of you and the entire family have made, you've really set the bar high for couples in Philadelphia to emulate.*
>
> Pennsylvania Governor Ed Rendell

PREFACE

Dan Tabas was one of the most successful entrepreneurs in the history of Pennsylvania. His entrepreneurial career spanned more than seven decades, from the nineteen forties to the first decade of the new millennium. During this time, he amassed a fortune in construction, real estate, hotels, dinner theaters, and banking. Along the way Dan pioneered new concepts in commercial construction and real estate development, turned a cow pasture in Downingtown into a goldmine, and transformed a tiny country bank with limited assets into a successful financial powerhouse.

Thanks to his vision and daring, and to his skills as a negotiator, a creative marketer, and a hands-on administrator, thousands of men and women were able to earn their livelihoods as either employees of, or vendors to, one of his many enterprises. Incredibly, he accomplished his remarkable achievements without a degree from Wharton or an MBA from Harvard. Instead, this son of a hard-working Russian-Jewish immigrant learned everything he needed to know about business the hard way — from the ground up.

But Dan Tabas was much more than a successful businessman: He enlisted in the Army during WW II and, after scoring in the top percentile on the aptitude exam, was chosen for pilot training by the Army Air Corps, distinguishing himself as a member of the generation of Americans that saved the world from fascism and then went to work to build the greatest nation the world has ever seen.

First and foremost, however, Dan was a family man. He and Evelyn, his beloved wife of almost fifty-five years, gave birth to six children, who in turn gave them twenty grandchildren and two great-grandchildren. Through the years, the Tabas clan has remained exceptionally close thanks to the expectations set for them by their extraordinary parents.

Dan was also a mentor and role model to dozens of men and women who, under his guidance, have gone on to carve out successful careers in real estate, banking, aviation and the hospitality industry. And he was a philanthropist who generously donated millions of dollars to causes that benefited needy children, the aged, education, health care, medical research, and the people of Israel.

On September 12, 2003, Dan Tabas passed away at the age of eighty. More than twelve hundred mourners attended his funeral. Tributes poured in from civic leaders, captains of industry, and Hollywood celebrities, yet during his remarkable lifetime Dan never forgot where he came from. Despite his wealth, he pumped his own gas, routinely put in fifteen-hour days, and answered his own phone. "He was just as comfortable in the company of workingmen as he was with jetsetters and tycoons," said Gene Turns, a trusted and longtime Tabas employee.

This is his rags-to-riches story, a historical record for all whose lives were touched by Dan Tabas. It is also a roadmap to success for anyone who hopes to turn a bright idea into a flourishing enterprise, or to truly understand what it means to be a devoted family man.

Dan's birthplace, 120 S. Massachusetts Avenue, Atlantic City, New Jersey

EARLY YEARS

My father started out washing soda bottles. He also sold tomatoes from a wagon in Philadelphia. My job was to contribute to the welfare of the family. When the Depression came along we lost our house. We had to start all over again.
Dan Tabas

Daniel Marvin Tabas was born in Atlantic City, New Jersey, on August 15, 1923. He was the youngest of Samuel and Esther Tabas' three children. While the blessed event, which took place in the front bedroom of his parents' home on Massachusetts Avenue, was greeted with unabashed joy, the rest of America was in deep mourning that day. Just weeks before the pink-cheeked and hazel-eyed baby boy made his debut, Warren G. Harding, the twenty-ninth president of the United States, died of an apparent heart attack in San Francisco during a cross-country train trip. It would take time for the nation of one hundred million to recover from the death of the popular president, or get used to its new president, Calvin Coolidge.

Sam Tabas with his children, Frances, Dan and Charles

What most Americans would not get used to, however, was Prohibition, the nationwide law that banned the production, sale and possession of all alcoholic beverages. It went into effect in 1920, giving rise to arguably the wildest ten years in American history, a decade characterized by flappers, speakeasies and ruthless gangsters like Al Capone, Lucky Luciano and Meyer Lansky.

Meanwhile in Germany, a disgruntled former house painter and army corporal named Adolph Hitler was beginning his march to power. Hardly anyone on this side of the Atlantic was paying attention. After all, the horrors of World War I, "the war to end all wars," were five years past. Besides, it was the Roaring Twenties and Americans were too busy learning the Charleston and the Shimmy, and taking in the marvelous technological advances of the 1920s that were making life better and more entertaining for everyone. The future looked bright indeed, and no one embraced it with more gusto than Sam (Pop-Pop) Tabas.

Sam Tabas, right, and his brother Abe, in Philadelphia circa 1910

Coming to America

Samuel Tabas arrived in New York Harbor on August 19, 1904, as Schmuel Tabachnik, a nineteen-year-old peddler's son from Russia. He was born on November 19, 1885, in the tiny town of Zabludava, in the province of Grodno Guberniya, which is located within of the Pale of Settlement, the one million square mile region that Jews were restricted to beginning in 1771 by Catherine the Great. The Pale, home to five million Jews in 1900, included the territory of what we know today as Poland, Latvia, Lithuania, Ukraine and Belarus (Belorussia).

Sam's mother called him "Mulke," which was derived from Schmuel, the Hebrew equivalent of Samuel. "We were poor," Sam would write years later in his moving memoir, *Mulke: A Reminiscence*. "By today's standards we could be considered to have been very poor." His boyhood home consisted of two rooms with a dirt floor. There was no indoor plumbing. Water for drinking and cooking had to be drawn from a well and carried in buckets which hung from a wooden yoke across the carrier's shoulders.

Despite the pogroms, poverty and the harsh living conditions, Sam recalled his childhood as a happy time during which he

Early Years

Sam Tabas thrilled to the sight of the Statute of Liberty when the steamer that carried him from Europe to America arrived in New York Harbor

was schooled in the traditions and rituals of Judaism at home and at the synagogue which was built from logs. Just after his tenth birthday, the family moved to Bialystok, then the largest city in western Russia. Sam began working full time at age thirteen, first as a weaver then as a worker in a rope factory, but he was much too smart, and too aggressive, to spend a lifetime toiling in a factory as an employee.

"The Russia of the Czars was not a pleasant place for Jews," Sam recalled. "There were very few opportunities for a Jewish boy to better his lot," so Sam went into business for himself. He put a sack on his back and gathered junk which he would then sell or trade. He was a go-getter, a natural-born entrepreneur, and after only one year had accumulated enough money to purchase his own horse and wagon. Still, he saw little chance of anything more than a subsistence living in Russia. "One could stagnate, make a living of sorts and get married and bring up a family," he explained. "But there was little chance for betterment, and I did not want to spend a lifetime of working to stay in the same place."

What's more, like all young men in Russia, Sam was obligated to serve in the Czar's army, which was at war with Japan. Jews were cannon fodder during the Russo-Japanese War of 1904-1905, and were routinely subjected to physical violence and persecution at the hands of their Russian officers. "There was no justice for Jews in the Czar's army," Sam remembered years later. So he and his best friend, Benjamin Tolinsky, decided to leave Russia and emigrate to the United States. It was an arduous and dangerous journey that began in the middle of a July night in 1904. "All the family walked to the edge of the town with us, my mother crying bitter tears and praying for our welfare," Sam recalled.

With Sam and Ben hiding in the wagon bed, Sam's father and his brothers, Abe and Morris, drove the young émigrés to the Polish border in the very wagon Sam had purchased for his junk business. It was a dangerous journey. Along the way they were harassed by Russian police and corrupt border guards who routinely rammed pitchforks into the wagon bed. Luckily, the young men were undetected and unhurt. After crossing into Poland, the two young men traveled on foot to Germany, then by train to the Belgian port of Antwerp where they booked passage to America.

Immigrants arriving at Ellis Island, circa 1904

As he stood on the steerage deck of the steamer that brought them to America, Sam was thrilled by the sight of the Statue of Liberty in New York Harbor. He was now a *freie mensch*, Yiddish for a free man, and he no longer had to fear pogroms, the Cossacks, or the *nagika*, the whip the Russian police were more than happy to wield, especially against Jews. The two travellers passed through Ellis Island where immigration inspectors made sure they were in good health and Americanized their names: Benjamin Tolinsky became Ben Tolin, and Schmuel Tabachnik became Sam Tabas. The two friends then headed to Philadelphia where Ben, who was engaged to marry Sam's sister Sadie, had relatives who had agreed to let them stay at their home at 232 Christian Street.

A Natural Born Entrepreneur

"My father came to America with nothing more than the shirt on his back, a dawn-to-dusk work ethic, and an awesome responsibility: As the oldest boy in the family, it fell to him to earn enough money to bring his father Lipka, mother Ida, two brothers and one sister to America, too," said Dan. "Even though he did not speak a word of English when he got off the boat at Ellis Island in New York harbor, Sam never doubted for a minute that he'd be able to. He believed with all his heart that he was in the *goldene medina*, the golden land, and anything was possible.

Two days later, Sam landed his first job in America as a bottle washer in a soda bottling plant. It lasted three days. For his labor, he was paid $2.25. During a weeklong search for another job, Sam decided once again that if he wanted to get ahead in America, he would have to go into business for himself, so he rented a pushcart for a

Sam said goodbye to his father, Moshe, and mother, Mindel, and journeyed to America. They joined him in Philadelphia one year later.

dollar-a-week and began hawking fruits and vegetables on the streets of South Philadelphia. It wasn't long before he was clearing the then-princely sum of one dollar-a-day. But Sam was always on the lookout for better opportunities, and when they knocked he was ready to open the door.

"I kept my eyes open and saw that there were opportunities in my original

Aerial view of the beach at Atlantic City and the famous Steel Pier circa 1920

business, which was rags and junk," Sam recalled.

In America junk meant much more than old rags and newspapers. It meant trading in scrap metal — iron and copper, which American industry couldn't get enough of thanks to an economy that was growing by leaps and bounds.

"My father took to the scrap metal business like a fish takes to water," Dan recalled. No one had to tell Sam Tabas that one man's junk is another man's treasure, and that discards had value. It was a concept that would form the bedrock of the Tabas family's enterprises for years to come. In less than two years, Sam had accumulated enough money to pay for his family's passage to America, and to rent a five-bedroom house for them at 905 Poplar Street. It even had indoor plumbing. "To us it was a palace," he proclaimed.

Meanwhile, Sam continued to grow his business aggressively. The Acorn Iron & Supply Company occupied a half block on Fifth and Clearfield Streets in Philadelphia, where Sam had installed a wagon scale and a machine to cut scrap. He also opened two locations in Atlantic City: A scrapyard and warehouse on Tennessee Avenue, as well as property at 2019 Arctic Avenue that included stables, a warehouse and a five-bedroom house. In 1912, Sam purchased an entire block on Tennessee Avenue where he built a three story warehouse, installed a floor scale and a truck scale, a machine for cutting scrap iron, a waste material-baling press, and a railroad siding. He also opened a scrap yard and warehouse in Chester, Pennsylvania, and he expanded his business into structural steel, erecting hotels and other buildings throughout the region. Before long, Sam Tabas was a major hotelier in then-bustling Atlantic City.

Thick with woods and lined with dunes, Atlantic City had been a resort since before the Civil War. Its cool ocean breezes in summer and proximity to major population centers in Philadelphia, Baltimore, Washington, D.C., and New York, made it a very popular vacation destination. During the 1880s the city's population exploded, and by 1912 it was drawing throngs of visitors to its hotels, its boardwalk (the world's first), floor shows and beauty pageants.

For Sam Tabas, who had arrived in America speaking no English and with little more than the shirt on his back, America really was the *goldene medina*. In just a few years he had become a pioneer in the recycling industry and a pillar of the business community. He was active in the Chamber of Commerce and a founding father of Atlantic City's burgeoning Jewish community, eagerly participating in fund raising for the resort city's first synagogue, the B'nai B'rith, and for the Young Men's Hebrew Association (YMHA).

Dan's parents Esther and Sam in their courting days

Sam had come a very long way in a short period of time, but his journey was just beginning. In November 1914, he married Esther Chapinsky, the American-born daughter of Russian-Jewish immigrants.

■ DANIEL TABAS

Mr. and Mrs. Samuel Tabas on their wedding day, November 1914

The newlyweds moved into a new home at 120 South Massachusetts Avenue where Esther would give birth to their first child, son Charles, in 1915. A second child, daughter Frances Pearl, was born in 1919. Daniel would arrive four years later.

During World War I, which began in 1914, but which the United States didn't enter until 1917, Sam's scrap metal business was essential to the war effort, supplying the metal needed for bullets and artillery shells as well as tanks and ships. "I became busier and busier," Sam recalled.

He had purchased a brass rod and tube extruding mill which sat on twenty acres of land in Downingtown, Pennsylvania. Sam didn't know it then, but that purchase would profoundly affect the Tabas family's fortunes for decades to come.

He also began acquiring residential and commercial properties in Atlantic City, apartment houses and stores, and providing structural steel for its landmark hotels including the Breakers, the Madison and the Ambassador. Around this time, too, he became a hotelier, operating the Stratford with one hundred rooms, and the Blackstone with five hundred rooms and a night club. Day-to-day responsibility for the hotels was placed in the hands of Charles who, although still in his teens, was mature beyond his years. "My brother in my eyes was always an older man," Dan explained. "When he was fourteen-years-old, he wore black clothes. He had an overcoat with a velvet collar. He always wanted to look five years older than he was. He never played ball. He never had a childhood."

Despite his age, Charles was a shrewd businessman. He proved his mettle when he undertook the task of refurbishing the Blackstone.

"My brother went to Philadelphia, to the-then famous Gimbel's department store," Dan recalled. "He bought an odd lot of wallpaper that Gimbel's had for five cents a roll that he bought from the boss himself, Mr. Bernard Gimbel. Then he hired a local paper hanger to paper the rooms for one dollar per room."

The refurbished Stratford reopened as a budget-priced hotel. Said Dan: "In those days rooms could be rented for about two dollars-a-night. The better hotels were getting six to eight dollars-a-night. Charles had five hundred rooms there, and if he could fill four hundred, he grossed eight-hundred-dollars a night. That was lot of money considering that a chamber maid earned about seventy-five cents a day. He'd earn about five-thousand-dollars over a season that lasted for about four months. That was a lot of money in those days."

Tragedy and the Great Depression

Charles learned the ins and outs of the business world from his father, but Sam Tabas's Midas touch couldn't guarantee good health for Esther. In 1926, while Dan was still a toddler, Esther succumbed to tuberculosis. Her passing left Sam with three small children to love and nurture alone. He rose to the occasion.

"My father was a great parent," Dan recalled. "We always had a hot breakfast and a good dinner, and always a Shabbat dinner every Friday night. He provided very well for us under the circumstances."

But Dan never knew his mother. "When I was one-year-old, she had been hospitalized for quite a time. I have no recollection of her. The only recollection I have is of my sister Frances who really raised me in those tender years."

It was Frances who filled the void left by Esther's passing. She was the one who made sure Dan wore gloves and earmuffs in winter, got his haircut regularly and had clean clothes to wear to school. Only four years older, she took on the role of mother to Dan, so it was especially hard on him when Frances was felled by a debilitating kidney infection she contracted at summer camp.

She bravely fought her illness for more than a year, but in the days before penicillin she had little chance to survive, and her health slowly deteriorated. When Sam learned that a top kidney specialist from New York would be in Atlantic City for a convention, Dan went with Sam to the Ritz Carlton to persuade the doctor to examine Frances who was in the hospital. "The doctor said he would examine her, but demanded $35 up front," Dan recalled. But hard times had fallen on America, and Sam did not have the money. On October 13,

Dan Tabas, age 3, with his older siblings Charles and Frances

1933, Frances succumbed. Her last words to Dan were, "Danny, take care of yourself."

Her passing left a void that would remain with Dan for the rest of his life. "It was a horrendous experience for me to comprehend," he said. "She was really my mother. I was only nine-years-old and she was thirteen."

Years later, Dan would say that the losses of his mother and sister were the defining moments of his life, that the tragedy taught him to cherish those we love and to have compassion for those who struggle with disease and handicaps.

Meanwhile, the Great Depression had the nation and the world in its grip. The energy and optimism that marked the Roaring Twenties gave way to despair. It started with the stock market crash of 1929, and quickly spread around the world. By 1932, more than thirty million Americans had no income of any kind. Masses of homeless and unemployed searched vainly for work or a handout. For most people, a vacation in Atlantic City had become out of reach.

The hard times also brought out the worst in people and nations. In January 1933, Hitler's march to power succeeded when he became chancellor of Germany and set about to implement his plans for world domination and the extermination of the Jews. Closer to home, an anti-Semitic priest from Michigan took to the airwaves on Sundays to broadcast fiery sermons to a listening audience of tens of millions. Known as "The Radio Priest," Father Charles Coughlin railed against communists and President Franklin Delano Roosevelt, but he directed his most venomous diatribes against Jews. The virulent anti-Semitism that Sam had left in Europe had caught up with him, and so, too, had poverty. It seemed that Sam's *goldene medina* had lost its luster.

With the collapse of the economy and his father's businesses, Dan pitched in. He was still in elementary school, a student at the Massachusetts Avenue School, but he demonstrated that, like his father, he had the makings of a successful entrepreneur.

For example, when the circus came to town, ten-year-old Dan sold ice cold Coca-Cola for five cents a bottle. A case of twenty-four cost eighty cents, which meant he earned forty cents for every case he sold,

Frances Tabas, right, with cousins Doris, left, and Ruth, on the beach at Atlantic City, circa 1932

DANIEL TABAS

14 year-old Dan at Hickory Run Camp in 1937

He also worked summers as a milkman's helper, arriving at Abbott's Dairy at three o'clock in the morning, seven days-a-week. He'd load a horse-drawn wagon with cases of bottled milk as well as sweet cream, sour cream, butter and cottage cheese. When the wagon was fully stocked, Dan walked the horse from the stable to the loading dock where he hitched it to the wagon. By the time milkman Dave Blum arrived at the dairy, everything was done and they could begin their daily rounds. They'd make two deliveries a day. It was hard work. But the job had a fringe benefit.

At first, Dave didn't want to hire young Dan. "I kept pestering him to hire me," Dan remembered. "But Dave kept telling me, 'you're too young, you're too little, you're too this, you're too that.'" Although he was only eleven-years-old, Dan already showed a remarkable instinct for marketing and a steely determination to succeed when he made the milkman an offer he couldn't refuse: Dan offered his services at no cost. He said, "Let me work for free for a couple of days, and I'll show you what I can do."

After only one day on the job, the milkman was so impressed with the youngster's ability and work ethic that he hired him. Dan's reward: A weekly salary of three dollars plus a fringe benefit. "When the milkman was away, I'd lift up the seat we were sitting on and take a half pint bottle of pure sweet cream and drink it. Boy did I love that!" Dan exclaimed.

Despite the meager wages, Dan was able to save enough money to purchase a reconditioned bicycle for nine dollars. "That bike was my first acquisition," he recalled

provided he brought all the bottles back. Said Dan, "If I lost a bottle it could cost me two cents. I didn't lose any bottles."

fondly. To safeguard the two-wheeler, he kept it next to his bed in his second floor bedroom even though it meant hauling the bike up and down a flight of stairs each time he wanted to ride it.

Despite the hard times, life in Atlantic City wasn't all work and no play for young Dan. In fact the resort city, with its hotels and attractions, was an exciting and stimulating place for an adventurous boy like Dan Tabas. He strolled the boardwalk every Sunday morning with his father, brother and sister, and he learned about showgirls.

"I was a very aware young man," Dan recalled, his hazel-blue eyes twinkling. "I was always very fascinated about one thing: The showgirls at the Globe Theater which was located on the boardwalk. It was only blocks from our hotel, the Blackstone. I remember as a young kid, two or three of us would climb up the fire escape and sneak in to the top balcony and look down and see these sparsely costumed young women displaying their impressive dancing skills."

And growing up in the resort city meant access to the attractions of the world renowned Steel Pier. Said Dan: "We didn't go on vacation. We lived in Atlantic City. From the time I was ten, I would fill a shopping bag with food, leave the house at around 9:00 A.M., and spend the whole day until midnight on the Steel Pier, twenty attractions for the price of one admission, which for kids was a quarter. I'd see three movies, the Hawaiian show, the diving horses, the aquatic divers, and the big bands—Benny Goodman, Glen Miller, Guy Lombardo. That was in the spring, summer and fall. In the winter, when it snowed, I would go sledding on the Boardwalk."

But even the glitz and glamour of the Garden State's popular resort city couldn't stave off hard times for the Tabases. By 1935, Sam was wiped out when Atlantic City's Guaranty Trust, like thousands of other banks from coast-to-coast, closed its doors. "My father lost all his money," Dan recalled. "And he exhausted all his efforts to earn money. The banks closed. They called it a bank holiday. My father and I stood in line all day, hoping the bank would reopen so we could get our money."

But that did not happen. Dan, who would one day become a banker himself, also lost his life savings. "I remember it perfectly. Thursday was bank day at school, and I deposited a nickel every bank day for years. I had fourteen dollars in the Guaranty Trust Company. I lost it all."

Sam also lost the only home he'd lived in since he returned from his honey-

DANIEL TABAS

Iconic photo from the Great Depression, by Dorothea Lange, 1936

moon with Esther in 1914. "Dan told me his father didn't have the money to pay the mortgage or even the interest on the mortgage," said longtime Tabas family friend George "Dewey" Laughlin. So at the age of thirteen, on the day after Dan celebrated his Bar Mitzvah, Dan, his brother Charles and Sam packed up all their worldly possessions and left Atlantic City. As he walked down the steps for the last time, Dan vowed that he would do whatever it took to make certain than no Tabas would ever again be forced from a home.

"Dan told me it broke his heart to leave Atlantic City," said Laughlin. "It was the only home he had ever known, but they had no choice, they were foreclosed. All they had was whatever they could squeeze into Sam's sedan plus enough money for gas to make the long drive to their new home," a row house at 5861 Malvern Avenue in Philadelphia.

Ed Johnston, a contractor who did work for Dan on his properties in Florida, recalled how profoundly that event impacted Dan. "That event and Dan's subsequent fear of debt had a tremendous impact on his life, affecting every financial decision he made."

"My father rented that house because we could move into it without having to pay the first month's rent, fifty dollars, upfront," Dan remembered. "He could pay it at the end of the month instead. My father didn't have the fifty dollars when we moved in, but he somehow managed to scrape it together by the end of the month." He did it by going back to his roots, collecting scrap from the streets of Philadelphia.

"They became scavengers," said Dewey Laughlin. "The three of them, Sam, Charles and Dan, spent the rest of the summer collecting items people were throwing away, and then they would sell them."

Before long Acorn Iron and Supply

Early Years

Aerial view of Acorn Iron and Supply, 915 N. Delaware Avenue, Philadelphia, serving industry for over 104 years; (inset) Moving structural steel beams to a building site

was back in business, operating from a new location at Delaware Avenue and Poplar Street on the Philadelphia waterfront. They worked hard. Dan drove the truck after school and on weekends, but hard times still had America in its grip, and habits acquired during the Great Depression would prove hard to break.

The economic collapse left Philadelphia and the entire Commonwealth of Pennsylvania in dire straits. Nearly twenty-four percent of Philadelphians were unemployed, while forty percent of workers in the rest of the Keystone State were jobless, too. The calamity created a health crisis – at one time during 1935, seventy-one thousand Philadelphians were reported to be suffering from malnutrition. Not only were working class people affected. Professionals and businessmen were affected as well. Physicians and attorneys found it difficult to collect fees. In 1935 members of the state legislature even reduced their annual pay from three thousand dollars to twenty-five hundred dollars. While President Roosevelt's New Deal alleviated suffering somewhat by providing direct relief payments to those in poverty who could not work, and jobs to the unemployed who could, ultimately it would be the need for Pennsylvania's products during World War II that would restore full employment in the state. But the years of the Great Depression scarred everyone who lived through them.

"You never forget," Dan noted. "For the rest of your life, you appreciate every little thing that comes your way. You never lose sight of that."

For example, his father gave him an allowance of twenty-five cents daily. "I spent ten cents of it every day," he said. "I bought a half of a package of Philadelphia cream cheese and three Uneeda biscuits. I ate that every day with a small container of milk. The three biscuits and cream cheese were a nickel, and the milk was a nickel." Dan managed to save fifteen cents every day, and his passion for saving money stayed with him his entire life, long after he had become a millionaire many times over.

Longtime friend Ed Tepper remembers driving from Downingtown back home with Dan one snowy winter night. Dan was behind the wheel of his Rolls Royce, which was low on gas. Said Ed, "Everyone who knew Dan well was aware that he would drive around looking for the least expensive gasoline, and that he only bought regular gasoline."

Dan pulled into a gas station to fill-up, but the station had only premium. The attendant pointed to a delivery truck that was filling the station's tanks with regular. He assured Dan that he would be able to purchase regular gasoline in twenty minutes. Even though the roads were becoming more and more treacherous by the minute, Dan chose to wait rather than pay the additional cost for premium gasoline.

Through high school, Dan worked with his father and brother in the family business, Acorn Iron and Supply. "It was the dirtiest work in the world," Dan remembered. "We took boilers out of basements. Every pipe was covered with asbestos, and I threw that stuff all over the place until the rooms were full of asbestos smoke."

Dan graduated from Simon Gratz High School in June 1941. He wanted to become an architect or a mechanical engineer. He had distinguished himself in the classroom and on the football field, but if Dan — his teammates called him "Duff" — and his classmates had high hopes for the future, they would have to put them on hold. With war raging in Europe and the Pacific, Congress had reinstituted the draft. Within six months America would be at war.

The War Years

Every generation enjoys good times and bad times, but for those like Dan, who grew up during the nineteen thirties and entered adulthood in the 1940s, life seemed especially perilous. By 1941, in fact, it was downright scary.

Dan Tabas during basic training, 1942

The Battle of Britain was underway as Hitler's mighty Luftwaffe, the German air force, rained bombs on London nearly every night. In Western Europe, the German army occupied Belgium, the Netherlands, Denmark and Norway. Paris fell to the Nazi invaders in 1940, and all across Europe Jews were either fleeing for their lives or being herded into death camps. Meanwhile Japan, Italy and

DANIEL TABAS

World War II: Dan Tabas was selected for pilot training

Germany had signed a military pact, forming an Axis they bragged would one day rule the world. But if the winds of war were blowing across Europe and the Pacific, at least for the summer of 1941, America was still at peace, and Dan "Duff" Tabas, was eager to expand his horizons.

He had a yen for adventure and an urge to travel. "I wanted to see the world," he recalled. "In those days, that meant the United States. My thoughts were to see this country." With his father's reluctant blessing, seventeen-year-old Dan, on the very day of his high school graduation, headed downtown, to the headquarters of the *Philadelphia Inquirer*, where he hitched a westbound ride to Harrisburg on one of the newspaper's delivery trucks.

"Even as a teen, Dan showed that he had absolutely no fear," observed former Deputy U.S. Attorney General Arnold Burns, a longtime friend and confidante. The solo journey took Dan across the Midwest and to California. When he ran out of money in Iowa, he landed a job repairing railroad ties. At Harold's Club in Reno, Nevada, he won two thousand dollars playing blackjack. And in San Francisco, young Dan had a very special encounter.

In San Francisco, I asked people what there was to see. They said I had to go to the top of the Mark, the world-famous Mark Hopkins Hotel. Waiting for the elevator with me was someone who looked very familiar. Finally, I got up the courage and asked, 'excuse me sir, are you from Philadelphia? You look very familiar.' As soon as I heard him answer I realized it was Humphrey Bogart. He invited me to join him for a drink. I had a Coke and spent the afternoon with him.

Upon returning from his cross-country journey, Dan enrolled at Penn State where he planned to study mechanical engineering, but on December 7, 1941, the Japanese attacked Pearl Harbor and

Early Years

reduced the U.S. Navy to smoldering ruins. America was at war.

"It happened on a Sunday morning," Dan remembered. "I was so frightened. They said the Japanese had landed in Pearl Harbor. I didn't know where Pearl Harbor was. I thought it was in Virginia. But we were very patriotic, and there was a feeling that everyone had to do their part."

And they did. Still reeling from the hardships of the Great Depression, and terrified by the world's unrelenting march to war, hundreds of thousands of young men flocked to recruiters to volunteer for the Army, Navy and Marines. Dan was one of them. After completing his freshman year at Penn State, he left school and enlisted in the Army.

He was sent to Fort George Meade in Maryland for basic training expecting to be assigned to the infantry. Instead, Dan caught the eye of his superior officers who saw in him the leadership qualities and physical and mental skills needed to become a pilot and an officer in the Army Air Corps. After completing training in Maryland, the Army sent Dan to Miami Beach and then to flight school at Bucknell University in Pennsylvania. By all accounts, he was an outstanding pilot, and the experience and the training sparked a lifelong passion for aviation and flying.

Not long after his discharge from the Army, Dan qualified for a civilian pilot's license. When the war ended in 1945, he was ready to soar.

Dan on the wing of his Globe Swift at Camden Airport

Whatever there be of progress in life comes not through adaptation but through daring
Henry Miller

Mr. Downingtown

What I got, I made, and I could have made it in Quakertown, Trenton or Boyertown. Downingtown didn't necessarily contribute. I was the benefactor. I gave to Downingtown
Dan Tabas

With his Army service behind him, Dan Tabas, like millions of other discharged GIs, rolled up his sleeves and rejoined the civilian work force. He was eager to get back to work with his father and brother at Acorn Iron and Supply, and he hit the ground running. It wasn't long before the twenty-two-year-old Army veteran demonstrated that he had what it takes to succeed as an entrepreneur.

As it had during World War I, the Tabas family's Acorn Iron and Supply played an important part in World War II, supplying scrap metal that was used for munitions, ships, planes and tanks that were so vital in the effort to defeat the nation's enemies.

One of Dan's first projects after his discharge was the launch of a new division dedicated to fabricating steel for the construction industry. Among his first assignments were steel supports for a balcony for the Bellevue Stratford Hotel's ballroom and an indoor ice rink at the Benjamin Franklin Hotel. As a result, by the end of 1946 Acorn was well positioned to participate in the post-war building boom by providing steel frames for major construction projects in the region. But before he could launch that division, Dan was put to work driving the company truck and gathering scrap. The truck he drove was an open-sided Mack truck, which didn't provide much protection from the elements. The tires in those days were solid rubber, not the pneumatic tires that are used today, which meant a very rough ride. The headlights and taillights were gas operated, which meant they were lit by opening each glass cover and lighting a flame. The truck's top speed was fifteen miles per hour, and it was prohibited from going through tunnels.

"In 1945, our Acorn business was doing very well when we got a phone call from Everett Hoopes, a prominent realtor in Chester County," Dan recalled. He had been home from the Army only a few months when Charles — Sam was away on his first ever vacation, a three month cross country journey by automobile — took the call. Hoopes told Charles that he had recently acquired twenty acres in Downingtown that Sam had purchased just before the United States entered World War I.

Short on cash during the lean years of the Great Depression, Sam had not paid the real estates taxes and the property was declared aban-

Aerial view of Downingtown 1949

doned. Hoopes was able to purchase it at a tax sale, but there was a catch: In order to obtain clear title to the twenty acres, Hoopes would have to go through an expensive legal procedure to clear up some title issues – unless Charles was willing to sign documents relinquishing all claims to the land. Hoopes explained that it would cost him about four hundred dollars to go through the legal processes, and he offered the Tabas family one hundred dollars to clear the title.

Intrigued, the brothers drove out to Downingtown on a Sunday afternoon to meet the realtor and look over the property. Hoopes took the brothers to see the twenty-acres which were bounded on three sides by roads and on the fourth by tracks belonging to the Pennsylvania Railroad. Located on the parcel were the ruins of three fieldstone buildings that once were the Cohansey Brassworks, the old rod and tube-extracting mill their father had purchased before World War I.

Mr. Downingtown

Dan recalled the story of his first land venture:

He showed us this plot of land which I remembered only vaguely from my youth. It had been a brassworks, and every now and then when I was a child we would drive out there on a Sunday from Atlantic City. It was a long ride, a three-hour drive, because back then the roads were very primitive. I never remember going there after I was thirteen. The walls had collapsed and the roofs had blown away in a twister some ten years earlier. I thought it would be a good idea to rebuild the buildings. I said to my brother, 'I'd like to reconstruct these buildings on the same foundations and with the same fieldstone that's lying here in the fields.'

Charles liked the idea, and instead of Hoopes paying the Tabases one hundred dollars, the brothers paid Hoopes four thousand dollars and repurchased the parcel. The deal they struck that day marked the beginning of their ventures in Downingtown.

Only forty miles west of downtown Philadelphia on the Lancaster Pike, Downingtown is nestled amid gently rolling hills in the picturesque Brandywine Valley of southeastern Pennsylvania. Blessed with many creeks and streams, early settlers built several mills in the area, which became known as "Milltown." Around the time of the American Revolution, it became

Dan conferring with the project engineer

known as "Downing's Town," in honor of mill owner Thomas Downing, an enterprising Quaker who emigrated from England in 1717. Following the War of 1812, "Downing's Town" officially became Downingtown. By the middle of the twentieth century, the borough had a new, albeit unofficial, name: "Danny Town," while throughout the region Dan Tabas became known as "Mr. Downingtown."

"It wouldn't hurt to call him that," observed Armand Taraschi, a former Downingtown Borough Council president and Chester County treasurer. "And," he added, "you can call the surrounding area Tabasville,"

In the Beginning

It all began with that phone call from Everett Hoopes. The ink on the paperwork that transferred title of the twenty acres back to the Tabases was hardly dry before Dan, despite Sam's misgivings, was hard at work on his first Downingtown project: Resurrecting the ruins that once were the brass factory. He hired a crew of masons and laborers and travelled there every few days from Philadelphia to give them instructions.

"No plans. No building permits. No ecology studies. We'd just go and build it," Dan said, recalling the era before red tape and environmental regulations.

Dan would arrive at the site either early in the morning or late in the afternoon and meet with the workers. He'd tell them, "put a window here, put a door there," and, like Phoenix rising from the ashes, there arose from out of the ground, on the original foundations and using the same materials that had been lying there, two magnificent fieldstone structures totaling fifty thousand square feet. Dan reminisced: "I remember when the buildings were going up, the rumor mill started in Downingtown. There were all kinds of rumors: General Motors was going to use them for an engine plant, or an aircraft company was going to use them to build fighter planes."

To add to the mystery, Dan had his own airplane, a Globe Swift, NC80661, a working replica of which sits on the front lawn at his home, Acorn Farm. In the late 1940s, he kept the single engine four-seater at the Central Airport in Camden, directly across the Delaware River from Acorn Iron and Supply in Philadelphia. "In five minutes I would be in my airplane. I would buzz those buildings in Downingtown at about fifty feet to see what work had been done. I'd see where the door openings were, or whether the stone was being laid right. This fueled speculation in the area, especially in the local newspaper. People wondered who the mysterious pilot was, and why he was buzzing the construction site."

They would find out soon enough, but in the meantime Dan kept them guessing. He had no idea what use the buildings would be put to. "None at all," he declared. "In those days no one would invest any money in property that you didn't have a lease for or a specific use for. It's very common now, but in those days no one built empty buildings, and no one built beautiful and charming industrial buildings. It was a risk, but we were risk takers."

Dan Tabas did take calculated risks and in doing so he pioneered a new concept in commercial real estate development: Constructing large commercial structures on speculation. The resurrected fieldstone buildings remained vacant for nearly a year until another out-of-the blue phone call, this time from a real estate broker in New York City, set off a chain of events that would forever alter the Downingtown landscape, the area's destiny, and the Tabas family's fortunes.

"He said, 'I have a prospect who heard about your buildings in Downingtown, and we

Acorn provided structural steel for a variety of projects in the Northeast and Mid-Atlantic states

Thanks to Dan, in 1949 Pepperidge Farm founder Maggie Rudkin began baking in Downingtown, starting with breads and expanding into cookies and turnovers. Pepperidge Farm employed four hundred workers and purchased ten thousand gallons of milk and a ton of butter every week from area farms.

would like to come see it," Dan remembered. "The broker traveled to Downingtown with a woman — red hair, middle aged, a very nice person. She was the famous Maggie Rudkin, but at that time her name didn't mean anything to me."

Rudkin was a Connecticut homemaker and mother who began making bread in the kitchen of her Fairfield farmhouse because one of her sons was allergic to the ingredients in commercially baked bread. That was in 1937, and before long Rudkin had perfected a delicious stone-ground whole wheat bread made from all natural ingredients. An article about her in the *Reader's Digest* spurred interest and she began selling loaves of bread through mail order. Encouraged by her family and friends, and her son's doctor, Rudkin also began selling her homemade, preservative free bread to local grocers. She named her company Pepperidge Farm, after the farm she and her husband Henry had purchased in 1926. The all-natural whole wheat bread was so popular with consumers, grocers were hard-pressed to keep their shelves stocked, so Rudkin began looking for ways to expand her business. After moving into larger facilities in nearby Norwalk in 1947, she set her sights on taking the Pepperidge Farm brand national.

"She'd heard about our fieldstone buildings and they appealed to her," Dan remembered. She was impressed not only by their beauty—"I'm in love with this building," Mrs. Rudkin exclaimed, but by the fact that she could purchase stone ground flour from mills in and around Downingtown that relied on water power. Dan said:

> *I didn't know anything about grinding flour on waterwheels. Sure enough there was a mill in West Chester where stone grinding was powered by waterwheels. We went over to see it, and it made her day. The ambiance of the buildings plus the availability of waterwheel milling were perfect for the image Rudkin wanted to project for the Pepperidge Farm brand.*

The two entrepreneurs struck a deal: Rudkin leased the thirty thousand sq. ft. building for ten years. Once it was up and running in 1949, Pepperidge Farm employed four-hundred Downingtown-area residents. Every week it purchased ten thousand quarts of milk and a ton of butter from local farmers. Evelyn and Dan visited Margaret Rudkin and her family at Pepperidge Farm in Connecticut, creating a personal bond that lasted for decades.

The Pepperidge Farm bakery was a shot in the arm for the local economy, but it was just the beginning. J.S. Woodhouse Company, a farm machinery distributor, leased the other building, and the Acorn Industrial Park of Downingtown was born. Dan would build five more buildings in the burgeoning industrial park whose blue chip tenants would eventually include Pillsbury Mills, Phillip Morris subsidiary Clary Multiplier, Burroughs/Unisys, Foamade Industries, the Beloit Corporation, and a Breyer's ice cream factory.

"There were no industrial parks anywhere before then," Dan observed. He was instrumental in pioneering the idea, one of a great many revolutionary changes sweeping across America in the years immediately following World War II. For example, in 1947 test pilot Chuck Yeager flew through the sound barrier. The color barrier that prevented African-Americans from playing major league baseball fell that year, too, when Jackie Robinson joined the Brooklyn Dodgers. With the greatest baby boom in American history underway (seventy-six million babies would be born in the years after the Second World War), one of the year's best-selling books was *The Common Sense Book of Baby and Child Care*. It was written by a pediatrician, Dr. Benjamin Spock, and it changed forever the way Americans raised their children.

Meanwhile, the country desperately needed housing, hospitals and schools to accommodate all the newcomers and their families. Communities would need churches and synagogues where they could worship, and resorts and restaurants where they could relax.

Dan saw it coming. While he was overseeing the construction in Downingtown, he was also the driving force behind the expansion of Acorn Iron and Supply into steel fabrication and structural steel for buildings. At his behest, and to accommodate Acorn's expansion, the Tabases purchased property along the Philadelphia waterfront, acquiring Piers Thirty-Six, Thirty-Seven, and Thirty-Eight on the Delaware River to house their structural steel business.

"I was the *shtarker*, the go-getter," he'd say, using a Yiddish word that means strong person, to describe his role in the family business. He proved it time and again, perhaps never more so than on the evening of July 5, 1947.

Love at First Sight

For the Fourth of July, Dan and his Army buddy, Joe Tracy, flew in Dan's Globe Swift to The Balsams, an elegant and historic four hundred room resort in Dixville Notch, New Hampshire, not far from the Canadian border.

"It was known as the Switzerland of America," Dan recalled. The famed resort had a long and glorious history. It first opened just after the Civil War as Dix House, a rustic twenty-five room inn which was named after the tiny town's founding father and first landowner, Colonel Timothy Dix, a patriot of the American Revolution who lost his life in battle during the War of 1812. In 1895 a wealthy Philadelphia inventor and industrialist named Henry Hale bought it and renamed it The Balsams.

While he was in the service, Dan met the then-owner of the hotel, Alvin Kallman. They had become acquainted thanks to Murray and Judy Rappaport of Amityville, on Long Island, New York. Towards the end of the World War II, Dan had been stationed at nearby Mitchell Field. The Rappaports frequently opened their waterfront home to G.I.'s for barbecues and fishing expeditions aboard their boat. Murray Rappaport was The Balsam's accountant. After the war, Kallman, who was interested in building a bomb shelter, called Dan and invited him to spend the Independence Day weekend as his guest at The Balsams.

In the aftermath of World War II, Americans feared retaliation for the devastating air war in Europe; all the major German cities had been bombed and even though the Allies had defeated Nazi Germany, many people were worried about revenge. Said Dan, "The prevailing feeling was if you're building a new house you should build a bomb shelter in the basement. Alvin kept bugging me. He said, 'I'm getting ready to build a home. I want a bomb shelter.'"

Dan tried to talk him out of it. "The last thing you want to do is build a bomb shelter out of steel," he explained. "If anything, it should be built from concrete." And he tried to convince the resort owner that building a bomb shelter in Dixville Notch was a foolish idea. "Who would want to bomb anything way up here?" he wondered. But Kallman was unconvinced. When he invited Dan to spend the Fourth of July weekend at the historic resort, Dan accepted.

"I had a pretty hot airplane, a Swift. There was no way I was going to pass up a chance to fly my plane to the mountains of New Hampshire for a free weekend," he recalled. So at the crack of dawn on July 4, 1947, Dan and Joe Tracy took off for New Hampshire from an airfield in Camden, N.J. They should have landed at an airport in Lanconia, thirty miles from Dixville Notch, but as they made their approach Joe said, "Let's fly up to the place and then we'll fly back to the airport." Dan agreed. Flying at treetop level, Dan buzzed the resort. "We saw this magnificent place nestled in the White Mountains, but we didn't make it back to the airport," he recalled.

Instead, they decided to land the Swift on the hotel's polo field. Said Dan, "There were men playing polo. When they saw us coming in for a landing they scattered. Two of them even fell off their horses."

It was a very impressive entrance, and it had all the guests at the resort wondering about the daring young men who had landed an airplane on the polo field. One of them was Evelyn Rome, a beautiful twenty-one-year-old teacher from New York City. Before the weekend was over, Dan Tabas would fall head-over-heels-in love with "Evy," and would unabashedly admit it was love at first sight.

After dinner the next night, Dan and Joe, dressed in tuxedos, went into The Balsam's night club. Said Dan, "Joe and I were just sitting at our table, drinking Budweiser beer in our tuxedos and listening to the band."

From the corner of his eye Dan noticed two couples who had entered the crowded, smoky room.

Dan met the love of his life, Evelyn Rome, in 1947

Rabbi Sigmund Rome would become Dan's father-in-law

To him they looked like they could be two married couples, but he wasn't sure. One of the women caught his eye. It was Evelyn. Dan couldn't take his eyes off her. He elbowed Joe, pointed to Evelyn and said, "I'm going to marry that girl."

"It seemed so ridiculous, we laughed," Dan would recall many years later.

At the time, marriage was the furthest thing from twenty-three-year-old Dan's mind. "I had a speedboat, a Cadillac convertible, and an airplane," he explained. "I lived at home, and I had all the romance I wanted on Saturday night. But all of a sudden, bang, I was in love."

Evelyn had been born in Brooklyn, New York, on January 30, 1925. She was the second of three children, all daughters, born to Dr. Sigmund J. Rome and Bluma Fine Rome.

Sigmund Rome was born in Zaleszczyky, Austria, in 1893. He came to the United States when he was only five-years-old with his parents, Hyman and Lena Sperling Rome. Hyman was in the fur business in Europe and opened a fur blending facility in Manhattan. Renowned for his singing, Sigmund studied music at Columbia University, graduating in 1917 with a degree in music. American-born Bluma had graduated from teachers college and was certified to teach school in New York. Evelyn's maternal grandparents, Russian immigrants Ida and Morris Fine, were the founders of M. Fine and Sons, a company they started in 1894 to manufacture work clothes. They began making long johns, military uniforms and overalls, and remained a family business for more than one hundred years.

Sigmund and Bluma married on July 6, 1919. A lifelong scholar, Sigmund earned a law degree from Brooklyn Law School in 1921 and practiced law from 1923 until 1936. He studied for the rabbinate at the Jewish Theological Seminary of America and was ordained in 1925. Two years later he founded the Tree of Life Temple in

Rabbi Rome and Bluma Rome outside their synagogue

Brooklyn. In 1934, he authored a *Comparative Study of Hebrew and Roman Criminal Law and Procedure*, a groundbreaking treatise that drew upon his knowledge of Jewish and Roman history, the Talmud and jurisprudence in ancient Rome. That year, too, he earned a J.S.D (Doctor of Law) from St. John's University in the New York City borough of Queens.

A highly regarded intellectual and a respected spiritual leader, he was well known for his dedication to civic activities like the United Jewish Appeal, the American Jewish Congress, where he was a member of the national executive committee, the United Palestine Appeal, and the Kings County Democratic Organization, which he served as vice chairman of its speaker's bureau. In 1934 and 1936 he was a delegate to New York State's Democratic Convention.

"Even though my father was always extremely busy, we were a close family," Evelyn recalled. "The whole atmosphere in our home was very spiritual." During the hard times of the Great Depression, couples would come to their residence to be married in Rabbi Rome's study. "Our lives were very different from the lives of our friends," Evelyn recalled. "We hosted small weddings in our home, and we'd all take part. My sisters and I were always on stage. We always had to have good manners, and we always had to be able to greet people and help with the ceremonies. There were many busy nights."

Sigmund Rome was also a brilliant and spellbinding speaker who was in great demand to make speeches and give invocations before all kinds of clubs and charitable functions.

Like her parents, Evelyn's interests were intellectual and spiritual. After graduating from Erasmus Hall High School in Brooklyn, she enrolled at Adelphi University in Garden City, New York. A year later she transferred to Brooklyn College from which she graduated in 1946 with a degree in psychology. She did her graduate work in early childhood education at The Cooperative School for Teachers at 69 Bank Street in New York City, which later became the renowned Bank Street College of Education.

Evelyn was staying at The Balsams along

with her older sister and brother-in-law, Dorothy and Dave Roberts. The trio had arrived at the resort earlier in the week following the June 29, 1947 wedding of Dorothy and Evelyn's younger sister Marilyn to Gene Koeppel, an automobile dealer from New York City. But Dan knew none of that when he first set his eyes on Evelyn.

Never at a loss for words, Dan quickly struck up a conversation with Evelyn and her sister and brother-in-law, and a man who sat nearby. Approaching the man first, Dan said, "Excuse me sir, I'm trying to play a game with my friend. I just drop a dollar bill, and all he has to do is catch it, but Joe can't do it. Would you like to try?"

The man couldn't do it either. He tried again, and still he couldn't catch the dollar bill. By this time, everyone at the table was eager to try, too. Before they could, Dan introduced himself. "By the way, I'm Dan Tabas," he said. "The man to whom I had been speaking introduced himself, and then he introduced the others: 'This is Mr. and Mrs. Roberts, and this is Miss Rome.' I thought to myself, 'MISS Rome! Wow!"

Dan and Evelyn danced for a while, then they left the nightclub. After changing into comfortable clothes, Dan borrowed a motorcycle and the young couple went for a spin.

While Dan was already in love, Evelyn needed courting. "She had many suitors," her sister Dorothy recalled. Nevertheless, she was interested in the dashing young man from Philadelphia. He had caught her eye, too.

"Dan was very different from the young men I had dated," she confessed. "Even though he was only two years older than I, he seemed much more mature, and he had an air of confidence about him that I found fascinating."

They had much in common. Both had both grown up in close-knit families grounded in Judaism and in service to others, but at the same time they were opposites. Where Evelyn was cultured and refined, Dan was rough around the edges. She had grown up nurtured and protected, while he was a streetwise young man whose early

Dan and Evelyn on their wedding day, December 4, 1948

years had been rocked by the deaths of his mother and sister and by the trauma of the Great Depression. Nevertheless, they were drawn together and made plans to see each other again.

The next day Dan and Joe flew back to Philadelphia, while Evelyn stayed on in New Hampshire. They wouldn't see each other again until two weeks later.

On Saturday July 19, Dan made the long drive from Philadelphia to 881 Eastern Parkway, a beautiful tree lined boulevard in Brooklyn that had been modeled after the magnificent Champs-Elysee in Paris, France.

"I parked the car, but couldn't find the address," Dan recalled years later. "Instead of a house, there was a synagogue there."

At first, he thought that Evelyn had given him a false address. She didn't, but she didn't tell her suitor that she lived above a synagogue. As Dan was about to get back in his car for the drive back to Philadelphia, his pilot's eye noticed the bulletin board in the garden in front of the temple. It read "Dr. Sigmund J. Rome, Rabbi." Relieved, Dan entered the synagogue. Once inside the family's living quarters above the sanctuary, he introduced himself to Evelyn's parents and was reunited with Evelyn. After the sun went down to end Shabbat, the couple drove to Coney Island for their first date.

Since the 1890s, Coney Island was where New Yorkers young and old from all walks-of-life went for summertime fun. Its magnificent beach, famed amusement parks like Steeple Chase and Luna Park, thrilling rides and carnival side shows and games drew millions of visitors from Memorial Day through Labor Day. By all accounts, the young couple had a wonderful first date, and by evening's end Dan was more determined than ever that he and Evelyn would walk down the aisle. Evelyn, however, was less certain, but Dan's charm, decisiveness and persistence would eventually win her over.

On their honeymoon, Dan and Evelyn visited with local residents near Kingston, Jamaica

DANIEL TABAS

Despite an on-again-off-again courtship that included a brief separation while Dan secretly volunteered his services as a pilot in Israel's fight for independence, Dan and Evelyn tied the knot on December 4, 1948 before two-hundred fifty guests at New York's Ambassador Hotel. As he had with his other daughters, Rabbi Sigmund J. Rome officiated at the ceremony that joined Dan and Evelyn together as husband and wife. Following the black tie reception, the newlyweds set off on a three-week honeymoon that took them to Miami Beach, New Orleans, Venezuela and the Caribbean. When they returned to Philadelphia, Dan and Evelyn and their newly acquired German Shepherd, Thumper, moved into a one bedroom, one bath apartment on City Line Avenue.

As the decade of the forties drew to a close, Dan's family life and business interests were flourishing. On October 5, 1949, ten months and one day after they were wed, Evelyn gave birth to their first child, Lee Evan Tabas.

That year, too, they blazed a new trail when

Lee Tabas is behind the wheel as Evelyn, pregnant, looks on

Dan and Evelyn with their first child, Lee Evan

they purchased eight acres on Mulberry Lane and Old Gulph Road in Haverford and began building their lifelong home, Acorn Farm. They were the first Jewish family to own property in the once restricted neighborhood.

Over the years Dan and Evelyn would add four more acres to Acorn Farm and five more children to their family: Linda Jane on June 22, 1951; Jo Ann on June 18, 1953; Carol Lynn on September 23, 1954; Robert Royal on January 3, 1956; and Susan Kimberly on February 2, 1963.

"Dan promised I would never regret marrying him," Evelyn said years later, adding, "I certainly never did."

Evelyn holds Susan, From left, Linda, Carol, Lee, Jo Ann, and Robert

Aerial view of Acorn Farm in 1949

Dan's vision and daring transformed Downingtown. The Downingtown Farmer's Market and auction is in the foreground. Also shown are the Tabas Hotel and the Downingtown Inn. The Downingtown Industrial Park and the Exton Industrial Park, other properties Dan developed, are nearby.

From little acorns mighty oaks do grow
English proverb

A Pasture Becomes A Goldmine

I was a speculator. I built huge industrial park buildings before I had tenants. I built housing units and a farmer's market. I always had confidence in my ability to make them succeed.
Dan Tabas

At the dawn of the new decade Dan, Evelyn and Lee Tabas moved into their new home, Acorn Farm on Mulberry Lane in Haverford. The move, coming as it did at the very beginning of the 1950s, exemplified Dan's boldness, his willingness to blaze new trails, and the growing prominence of the Tabas family in the region. Even though he was still in his early twenties, Dan was an imposing man with a strong voice and a tenacious old-world work ethic, an ethic that was just as sturdy as the structural steel with which he built buildings. Nick Randazzo, CFO of Acorn Iron and Supply, has worked shoulder to shoulder with three generations of the Tabas family over four decades. He said, "No one worked harder than Dan. He was the sparkplug, the mover and the shaker. Dan had vision."

While Sam and Charles devoted most of their time to overseeing Acorn Iron and Supply on the riverfront in Philadelphia, Dan, more likely than not, could be found in Downingtown, supervising the Tabas family's growing operations in the Chester County mill and farming community which included the Exton Industrial Park on Tabas Lane as well as the Downingtown Industrial Park.

Longtime housekeeper Ruth Brown with Jo Ann, Lee and Thumper

With the end of the Second World War, economic and cultural forces were set in motion that profoundly changed the American landscape. For one thing, a tidal wave of pent-up demand for consumer goods that had been in short supply during the Great Depression and the war years swept the nation. Low cost G.I. mortgages allowed returning veterans to buy homes in the suburbs with very little money down. They needed automobiles to get to and from their jobs in the city, and everyone wanted a TV set. Nineteen million were sold in 1952, the year Dan, as president of Tabas Enterprises, the family-owned business, launched an ambitious new project — the Downingtown Farmer's Market and Auction. Just forty-six miles from Philadelphia, it provided a memorable and worthwhile destination for weekend drives into the countryside.

Dan boldly predicted that the farmers market would revolutionize buying and selling habits in the area, which it did by offering merchants low rent while customers received the benefits of retail prices that were thirty to forty percent lower. Located on fifty acres on the Lancaster Pike (Route 30) that the Tabas brothers purchased for twenty thousand dollars, it was an instant success when its doors opened for the first time on November 20, 1952. Sixty thousand men, women and children visited the market during the grand opening weekend. The next day the local newspaper, *The Downingtown Archive*, reported that the opening created "the biggest traffic jam in the area's history" with cars "lined bumper to bumper three deep as far west as Coatesville and as far east as Exton."

The scene was reminiscent of a full house at Municipal Stadium for the Army-Navy game…In the town proper merchants benefited from the traffic jam and overflow crowd. Town Motors sold six cars Friday evening, the most in that period of time in their history. The Department Store had a big evening as did Morris Kaufman, Western Auto and the restaurants.

On all sides there were compliments for the way the opening was handled. All of southeastern Pennsylvania was covered in newspaper and radio advertising, and nothing was omitted in actual on the spot arrangements from parking attendants to a nurse-staffed first aid room.

Dan had covered all the bases. He provided parking for fifteen thousand cars. He required merchants who rented booths at the farmers market to offer an unconditional, no questions asked money back

A Pasture Becomes a Gold Mine

guarantee. What's more, there were more than thirty thousand Christmas trees on hand, "probably the largest selection to appear in this area," the *Northern Chester County Herald* noted.

In the weeks that followed, thousands of families flocked to the Downingtown Farmers Market and Auction, drawn not only by Dan's vision but by his flair for marketing and his burgeoning talent for showmanship. The market was open on weekends until midnight, and shoppers could purchase everything from apples to window treatments. An entire section was devoted to Amish merchants who sold their homemade products like shoo-fly pie and fastnact, a sugar-dusted doughnut made from potato flour, and pretzels. The Downingtown Farmers Market and Auction is where Anne Beiler launched Auntie Anne's Soft Pretzels. It grew into a nationwide chain with hundreds of locations, and Dan was very proud that he had a hand in giving Auntie Anne her start in business.

Not surprisingly, Dan greatly admired the Amish merchants. "They're very good business people, very productive and very wholesome," he said. "They're most conscious about making every penny count. They don't waste a thing and they

Artist's rendering of the Farmers Market and Auction

DANIEL TABAS

Dan's creative advertising included contests, specially priced items, giveaways and celebrity appearances which helped drive business to the popular farmer's market

have very strong convictions." That admiration sparked an act of kindness not long after the market opened its doors, according to another local paper, *The Daily Local News*, which reported the following:

> The Downingtown Farmers Market and Auction wired $27.95 to the sheriff of the county jail of LaGrange, Indiana, to pay the fine and affect the release of Mrs. Melvin Schrock, a 35-year-old Amish woman, who was arrested for driving her horse and buggy without a license.
>
> Payment of the fine by Mrs. Shrock would have been contrary to the teachings of her religion, therefore she has been serving out the sentence of 27 days in jail.

When the Amish woman's plight came to the attention of the Tabas brothers, they didn't hesitate. "We thought that Mrs.

A Pasture Becomes a Gold Mine

Shrock should be home with her husband and children getting ready for the holidays, so we paid the fine," Dan recalled years later. It was an early act of generosity, one of many that would be a common occurrence for Dan and Evelyn in the years ahead, and it demonstrated that the Downingtown Farmers Market and Auction was much more than a place to shop. That's because Dan was always mindful of his civic responsibilities and concerned about the well being of children. He made certain that a weekend never went by without scheduling an activity to benefit kids and the community. For example, cartoon characters like Donald Duck with his "voice" Clarence Nash were frequently on-hand to entertain youngsters, as was TV cowboy Rex Trailer

Pretzel makers prepare the dough at Auntie Anne's soft pretzels, which got its start at the Downingtown Farmer's Market. Today, Auntie Anne's is worldwide with over 1100 locations in 44 states and 22 countries

Shoppers could find everything from apples to window treatments at the Downington Farmers Market and Auction

and his horse Gold Rush. The Future Farmers of America and the local 4-H Club were given booths at no charge, as was the American Red Cross and many other non-profit civic organizations.

There were fireworks on the Fourth of July and wonderful giveaways like the beautiful pony that eight-year-old Charlotte Demko of Honey Brook won in 1955 — her prize for taking first place in a coloring contest that was sponsored by the Downingtown Farmers Market and Auction. Other attractions included the circus, which visited periodically through the years, custom car shows, country-and-western concerts, an indoor trout fishing stream and personal appearances by the "the world's tallest woman" and "the world's fattest twins."

But getting a colossal project like the Downingtown Farmers Market and Auction off the ground wasn't easy. Originally scheduled to open in September 1952, weather and labor problems delayed the opening by nearly three months. But Dan, as he always did, persevered. It was a trait that he demonstrated when he convinced a skeptical milkman to hire him for the summer; one that he would demonstrate again and again through the years as he made his mark in the business world.

"He never met an obstacle he couldn't overcome," said longtime employee Gene Turns. Not even the devastating fire in 1976 that destroyed much of the market could stop him. When it first opened in the fall of 1952, the farmers market encompassed sixty-two thousand square feet and housed one hundred twelve merchants. The rebuilt market was bigger and better than ever when it reopened, with one-hundred-twenty thousand square feet and nearly two hundred tenants, plus an open-air flea market. By all accounts it was the biggest farmer's market in North America. "The man didn't succumb to stress," said son-in-law Ken Tepper. "He was always the strongest person in the room, no matter what the situation."

Even if Dan Tabas had never done anything more than build the industrial parks in Downingtown and Exton and the farmers market, he would have left an indelible mark on the region. In 1962, *the Philadelphia Inquirer* looked at the growth in Downingtown:

Tabas operations have transformed Downingtown into a boom town. Some 1500 persons are employed by Pepperidge Farm. Other major industries in Tabas-owned buildings include Beloit Eastern Corporation, paper making machinery which employs one thousand; the Millprint Division of Philip Morris, Inc., nine hundred employed, and Downingtown Paper Co., five hundred employees. Daniel Tabas points out that location plays a big part in the Downingtown success story since it is served by both the Pennsylvania and Reading Railroads as well as the Pennsylvania Turnpike and U.S. 30.

Bigger and Better

But Dan Tabas was never a man content to rest on his laurels. Around the time that he began thinking about the farmers market, he was already well along on another ambitious project, one that would go a long way toward establishing him as a leader in the hospitality industry. It would also solidify his reputation as one of America's most innovative hoteliers, and the Tabas name became synonymous with year round vacation travel, fine dining, PGA championship golf and world class entertainment.

The Downingtown Inn Golf & Tennis Resort

In late 1952, and for much of his life thereafter, Dan Tabas was a very hungry man. He was hungry to grow the Tabas family's business interests — leasing buildings to blue chip companies in the industrial parks he built in Downingtown and Exton, but he was frustrated because there were no quality restaurants in the area.

"We'd bring prospects here and we'd spend the morning talking business," he said. "Then I'd want to take them to lunch but there was no place to go. All that was there was a dinky diner in town and a great homemade ice cream place and dairy farm up the road called The Guernsey Cow." Dan decided to solve this problem by building his own restaurant. He bought a farmhouse, the 1796 Ashbridge Mansion, and the adjoining one hundred acres, for one hundred thousand dollars.

It was his intention to convert the venerable mansion into Downingtown's first world-class restaurant, which would be called 1796 House. But there was a hitch: After remodeling had been underway for months, Dan learned he would not be able to obtain a liquor license. "We were three quarters finished when some guy stopped

A Pasture Becomes a Gold Mine

by one day to see what we were doing," Dan remembered. "I told him and he said we'd never get a liquor license for the restaurant because there was a quota on them, and we couldn't buy one."

As Dan would learn, liquor licenses were tightly regulated by the township, and there already was a bar in the area. In fact it was located directly across the road from the Ashbridge Mansion. At first he was stymied, but Dan learned that his new venture could serve liquor if it could qualify for an inn license. To qualify, it would need at least twelve rooms which could be no smaller than forty-two square feet each. Each room had to contain at least one bed and running water. So Dan went back to the drawing board and drew up new plans for the second floor with the idea of furnishing twelve tiny rooms with surplus army cots and sinks.

He never intended to actually rent them, but with the encouragement of his brother Charles, Dan built an addition to the mansion and created the Downingtown Motor Inn. Its rooms were four star, the restaurant was top notch, and the Inn did very well, attracting visiting businessmen as well as tourists out to explore the Amish countryside until the state of Pennsylvania erected a highway bypass that diverted traffic away from the Inn. When that happened, business died.

Dan recalled: "I was a speculator. I built huge industrial park buildings before I had tenants. I built housing units and a farmer's market. I always had confidence in my ability to make them succeed." But the day the bypass opened, Dan's confidence ebbed. "We lost a third of our occupancy rate," he recalled. "We had a beautiful hotel and no business as everyone went around us. The place was like a morgue." To Dan and Evelyn's daughter Linda, "it was as if a spigot had been turned off."

Dan considered offering the Inn to the state to use as a hospital, but decided to roll the dice yet again; he placed an advertisement in the *New York Times*: "Three days, two nights, $29.75 complete" plus a tour of the nearby Pennsylvania Dutch countryside". He even bought a double-decker London bus. His marketing genius turned the tide as New Yorkers and others came to visit the Amish country. Many guests brought their golf clubs, too.

"We were sending as many as two hundred guests a day to a nearby golf course, it didn't make sense" Dan said. "If

One of the first brochures to advertise the Downingtown Motor Inn which later became the popular Downingtown Inn Golf and Tennis Resort with more than seven hundred rooms

A Pasture Becomes a Gold Mine

the people wanted golf that much, then we'd give them golf, so we bought the farm next door and turned it into an eighteen-hole golf course."

The farm's historic main house, once used by U.S. President Woodrow Wilson as a vacation retreat, became the pro shop, while the old horse barn was converted into the clubhouse, and an old ice house was converted to a two-bedroom cottage that would one day house Hollywood legend Mickey Rooney. Next to it Dan built a pond and stocked it with trout. Every afternoon at four a hotel worker, armed with a fishing net, retrieved trout and made a beeline back to the kitchen where they were prepared for dinner.

After starting out with only twelve rooms, Dan added twenty more, then he added another one hundred twenty. When he was done, there were more than six hundred guest rooms — "the rooms are comfortable and big. Big, that's the way Dan Tabas likes things done," trumpeted a 1970 review in *Philadelphia Magazine.*

Dan had transformed the motor inn into a year round, world-class resort on five hundred lush acres. It offered a plethora of amenities including a spa, indoor and outdoor swimming pools, tennis courts, horseback riding, a game room, ice skating rink, a PGA accredited championship golf course as well as a miniature golf course, and a magnificent dinner theater that featured wholesome Broadway shows like *Oklahoma, The King and I, Come Blow Your Horn,* and *How To Succeed In Business Without Really Trying.* Four orchestras were on hand to entertain guests.

In addition to families on vacation, the Inn did a booming convention business, hosting everything from the Teen Model of America conference to the American Funeral Directors' convention. "Those guys were really cards," Dan told an interviewer. "One of them kept following me around the whole week he was there, saying, 'Can I show you something in knotty pine?'"

From his office overlooking the Inn's indoor ice-skating rink, Dan summed up his hotelier's philosophy for the interviewer: "The day you stop improving and enlarging your facility to make it better for your guests is the day you ought to get out of the hotel business. You've got to keep up. There's always something new coming along, and if you want to please your guests you certainly want to give it to them."

To keep the people coming from far and wide, Dan brought in the biggest name entertainers of the 1960s and 1970s, head-

DANIEL TABAS

liners like Eddie Cantor, Henny Youngman, Carol Channing, Lana Turner, London Lee, John Raitt, Danny and the Juniors, Bobby Rydell, Tony Martin, Al Martino, Joan Rivers and the legendary Mickey Rooney, and he promoted the Downingtown Inn heavily in major urban centers like New York, Philadelphia, Baltimore and Washington.

Lou Reda was one of the talent managers who booked acts into the Downingtown Inn. One of them was The Amazing Kreskin, who billed himself as "the world's foremost mentalist." Kreskin mystified audiences with demonstrations of extra sensory perception and regularly drew sellout crowds to his performances at the Downingtown Inn.

Now an award-winning documentary film producer, Lou recalled Dan's flair for showmanship and marketing. He remembered suggesting that Dan book Kreskin. When the first show sold out, Dan decided to put on a second show, which sold out, too. From then on, whenever Kreskin appeared on *The Tonight Show with Johnny Carson* and *The Mike Douglas Show*, he made it a point to mention his upcoming appearances

A Pasture Becomes a Gold Mine

at the Downingtown Inn and his good friend, Dan Tabas.

"Dan Tabas turned a cow pasture into a gold mine," said musician Ray Carr, whose jazz orchestra regularly played the Downingtown Inn during the 1960s. "When he first started there was nothing, but before long they came out by the busload."

To keep them coming, in 1965 Dan teamed up with one of the biggest stars of the era, Hollywood superstar Mickey Rooney. The Downingtown Inn was renamed "Mickey Rooney's Downingtown Inn Golf and Tennis Resort." They had met in the Army then renewed their friendship when Rooney starred in *Girl Crazy* at the Valley Forge Music Theater.

Rooney's parents had been stage actors, and he had made his acting debut when he was only fifteen months old. Between 1927 and 1933 Rooney starred in fifty films playing Mickey McGuire, a comic-strip character. Legend has it that Walt Disney named Mickey Mouse after Rooney who, as a child actor, attended Hollywood's School for Professional Children where he first met Judy Garland. The two child stars appeared together in more than a dozen films. In 1935, Mickey gave a critically acclaimed performance as Puck in

Shakespeare's *A Midsummer Night's Dream*. Other memorable performances included movies like *The Adventures of Huckleberry Finn* in 1939, and *National Velvet* in 1944, but when he returned to Hollywood after World War II, Mickey found it difficult to land starring roles so he went on tour crisscrossing the country playing nightclubs and theaters.

Dan Tabas and Mickey Rooney entered into a business relationship whereby Mickey lent his name and persona to the resort and appeared in commercials in exchange for an equity interest. The relationship proved to be a brilliant marketing strategy, and it lasted through the sixties, seventies, eighties and nineties, while their friendship lasted even longer.

"God gave Dan enormous drive," the Oscar-winning actor said. "He never thought of failure, instead he always said 'I can do it,' and anything he did turned out to be successful."

When he wasn't in Hollywood making a film, or in New York appearing on the Broadway stage, Rooney could be found at the Downingtown Inn contributing his boundless energy and enormous talent to the dinner theater's productions. He also mingled with the guests and played lots of golf.

It was a sunny June day in 1969, and Dan and Mickey were enjoying a round of golf at the Inn. They were on the back nine when a mob of reporters came running towards them with the sad news that legendary singer Judy Garland, Mickey's longtime costar and beloved friend, had died from an overdose of barbiturates in London. Immediately Mickey, with Dan at his side, left the golf course and headed for New York to console Judy's family.

While Mickey Rooney's name graced the Inn's marquee, there was never any doubt that the Tabas family was in charge. The Downingtown Inn was a family business, and Dan and Evelyn were the hosts.

"Dan was the commander-in-chief, and Evelyn Tabas was the first lady," said longtime employee Gene Turns, the director of maintenance for the Downingtown Inn and all of the Tabas properties. "He never made a move without consulting her, and she was always at his side to smooth ruffled feathers."

That's because Dan, a hands-on boss, could be very demanding. He was a perfectionist, and the pressures of running a world-class resort were enormous. Depending on the season, there were as many as four hundred employees to supervise and thousands of guests to entertain,

A Pasture Becomes a Gold Mine

amuse and feed.

"Dan was a gourmet, and he always wanted everything to be perfect for his guests," recalled Uwe Blessman, the Inn's longtime head chef.

Blessman worked at a famous hotel in Istanbul, Turkey before coming to the United States. When Dan and Evelyn met him he was working at another establishment but they were so impressed with the Swiss-born chef's culinary skills, they prevailed upon him to pack up and move to Downingtown in 1962 to run the Inn's kitchen. In 1981, he would become the head chef at the Tabas Hotel.

"Dan wanted the very best quality from suppliers, nothing but prime, and he would get upset if he didn't get it," Blessman recalled.

It wasn't unusual for Dan to give a supplier a piece of his mind, and he could be hard on employees, too. "If you did a perfect job you were okay, but if not you could be in trouble," said Blessman. "But he was always fair, and only dismissed employees in very extreme cases." Uwe added, "He was very generous to those who worked for him, which is why many of the people who have worked for Dan through the years would walk through a wall of fire for him."

Blessman was far from the only employee recruited from abroad. Travel arrangements were made by Louise Golden, Dan's longtime executive assistant, who became an authority on visas and immigration. On one of dozens of trips to Europe, Dan and Evelyn met Vitale Demonti. They hired him to work in the dining room. He eventually became a maitre d' at the Downingtown Inn

"I remember when I met Mr. and Mrs. Tabas at a hotel in London," Vitale recalled. "They talked to me just like I was a member of the family. After just a few minutes Mr. Tabas told me I had the job. 'I'll send you an invitation. Take it to the American Embassy in Zurich and you'll get a visa to come to Downingtown.' Mrs. Tabas was so graceful and pleasant; she made a big impression on me that day."

Two months later, Vitale arrived in Downingtown. "Mr. Tabas arranged a car for me, a nice Mustang convertible. I was in heaven," he said. "The pancakes — I never saw them in Europe, and the prime rib, so big they would fall over each side of the plate. Mr. Tabas always visited and asked how I was doing. He liked to be served by me, and he complimented me on how smooth [my service] was, and he always introduced me to his friends, which made me feel that I belonged to the family."

He added: "There was no problem Mr. Tabas could not solve. I was aware that at times he was difficult for some people to deal with, but to be a successful businessman you can't always be Mr. Nice Guy."

Musician Giuliano Salerni was another European the Tabases found during one of their trips to Cannes on the French Riviera. The twenty-seven-year-old pianist and his band were appearing at the posh Hotel Martinez where the Tabas family was staying. They met at five o'clock one morning, while going through the hotel's revolving front door.

"I was returning from a party, and Dan was dressed in short pants," Giuliano

Louise Golden, longtime executive assistant to Dan Tabas

Double-decker London bus took Downingtown Inn guests on tours of Philadelphia and the Amish country.

recalled. "He told me he wanted the band in Downingtown as soon as possible."

Nine months later, the band was appearing at the Downingtown Inn. "Dan came up a name for us – The Monte Carlos," Giuliano said. "He even advertised us as having been the favorite band of Prince Rainier and Princess Grace of Monaco."

It was a clever marketing strategy, especially in Philadelphia, Grace Kelly's hometown. Kelly, a Hollywood superstar in the 1950s and regarded as one of the most beautiful women of the twentieth century, married Prince Rainier of Monaco in 1956, in a ceremony that was broadcast around the world.

Dan arranged television appearances for the Monte Carlos. He introduced them to show business luminaries, and he stayed in touch with Giuliano after the musician

■ DANIEL TABAS

Dan with his good friend and Hollywood legend Mickey Rooney, who fondly referred to him as "Uncle Dan"

returned to Europe. An earthquake in 1997 damaged Giuliano's home in Umbria, a region in Italy. Dan offered to bring Giuliano and his entire family to Philadelphia and booked him into his City Avenue hotel. Said Giuliano, "Dan showed me his big heart. I honestly loved that man."

"There never was a man like Dan Tabas," declared Joe Campbell, who would one day become the president of Dan's bank, Royal Bank America. According to Joe, who began working at the Downingtown Inn as a busboy at age fourteen, and worked side by side with Dan Tabas for many years afterwards, "He was demanding, but his demands only made you better."

And Dan was generous. He paid for employees' children to go to college, and he bought cars – Cadillacs – for all the top managers. "If he questioned something you did, he respected you if you stood your

A Pasture Becomes a Gold Mine

ground," Campbell remembered.

While Dan was a generous employer, he was also a generous and innovative hotelier. One year, he even paid for gas for his guests. It was a marketing strategy aimed at overcoming the gasoline crisis of 1973, when OPEC, the international oil cartel, turned off the spigots and forced Americans to wait in long lines at service stations to fill up their gas tanks.

Fearful that they wouldn't be able to buy gas for the drive home, Dan came up with the idea of giving every guest a free tank on checkout. With Mickey Rooney taking to the airwaves saying, "Come to my place — I'll fill your gas tank free," the giveaway worked. While other resorts saw their vacancy rates increase, the Downingtown Inn remained near capacity during the crisis.

The Inn offered the modified American plan, which meant for a set price guests enjoyed accommodations, access to all the facilities and two meals a day. With gasoline less than forty cents a gallon, the median cost of a home seventeen thousand dollars, and annual tuition at an Ivy League college under three thousand dollars, it was a popular destination for families, and the Tabas children were expected to be there, too, only they were there to work.

"We were always expected to contribute," remembered Lee Tabas, who, among other tasks, worked side-by-side with Uwe Blessman in the kitchen.

"We were required to get our hands

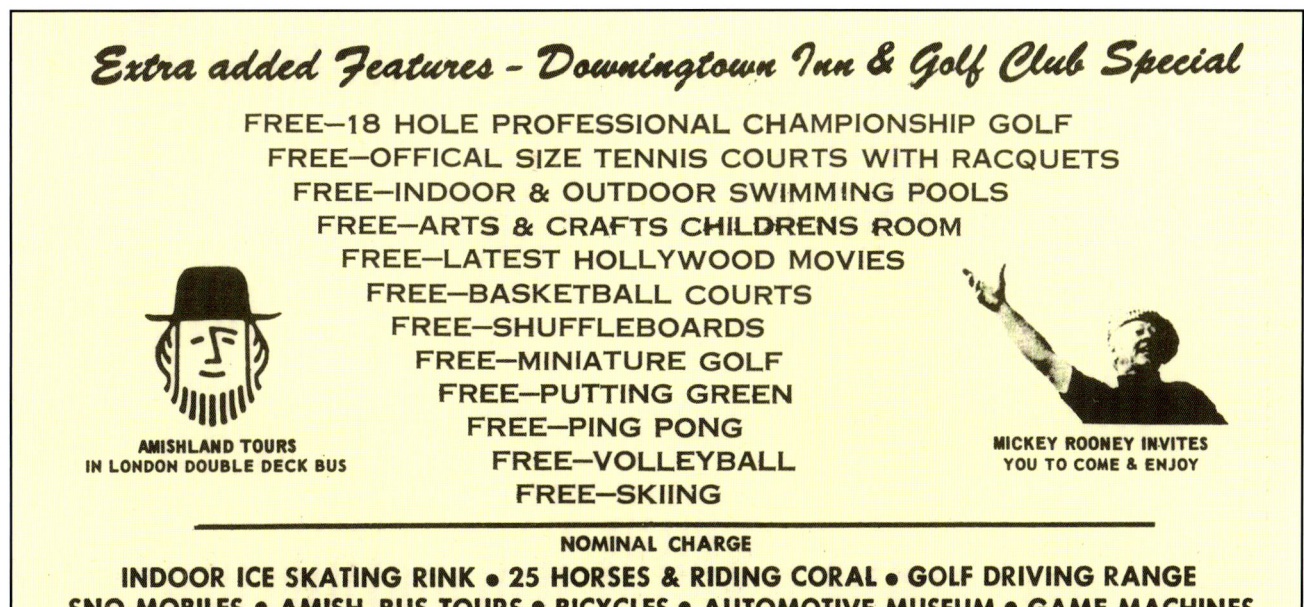

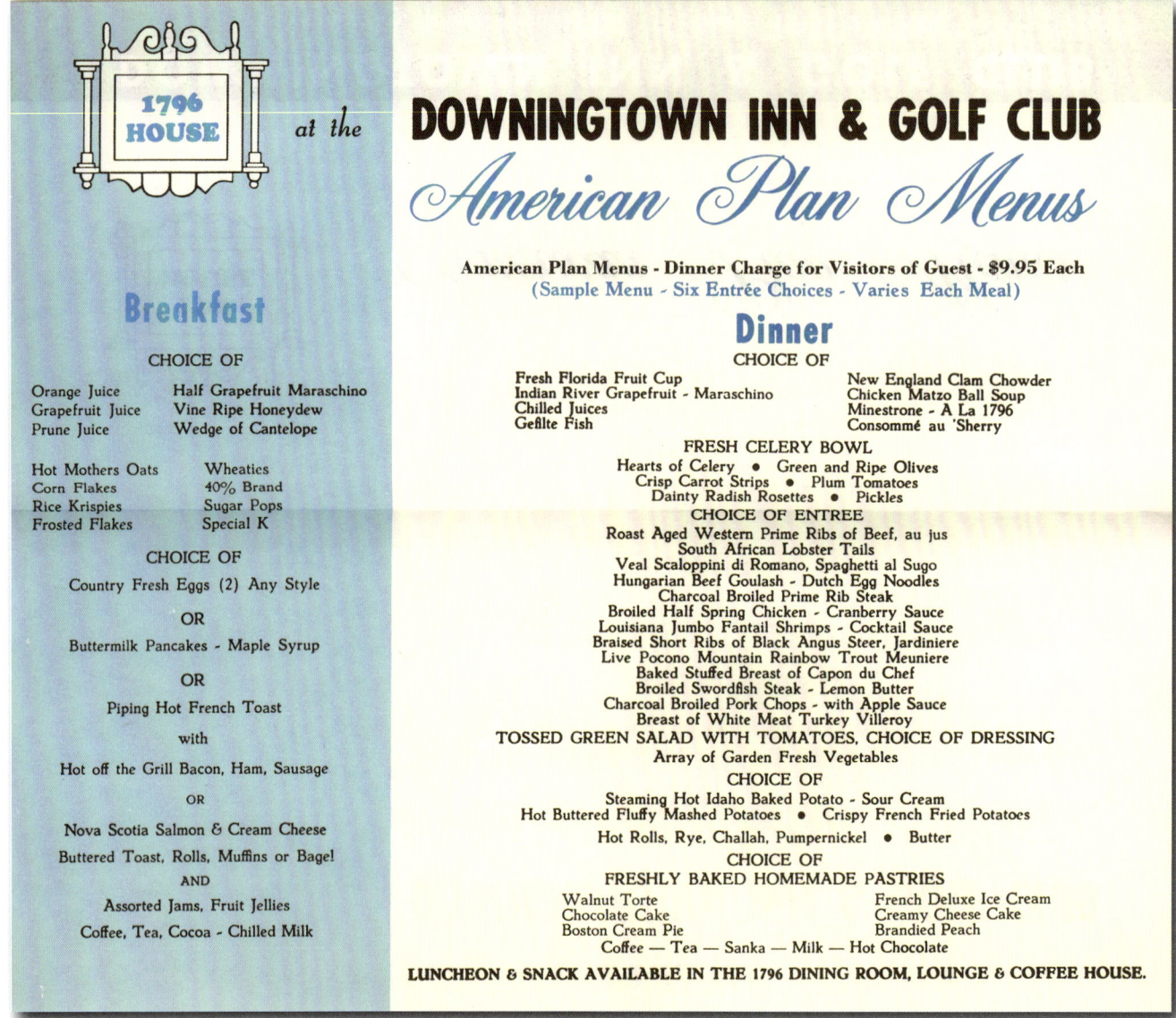

dirty," recalled his sister Carol, who bussed tables in the coffee shop, worked in the game room as well as the kitchen, and also worked as a restaurant hostess. Even when they were older and living away from home during their college years, the Tabas children would come home on weekends and holidays to work at the Inn.

"I never went out on a Saturday night because I had to work," Linda Tabas recalled, Dan and Evelyn's second child and oldest daughter. New Year's Eve was no exception – the Tabas children had to work.

Linda remembers receiving a letter from her father while she was an undergraduate at the University of Pennsylvania. In it, Dan wrote of her "obligation to the hand that feeds you," and he reminded

Linda that she was expected to work weekends at the Downingtown Inn.

Her brother Robert worked as a busboy, dishwasher, and kitchen manager at the Downingtown Inn. In later years, he worked as kitchen manager at the Riverfront Dinner Theater and as Master of Ceremonies at the City Line Dinner Theater. As a teen, Linda dispensed change in the game room and worked as an arts-and-crafts counselor, and eventually on the door of the nightclub. Years later, she served as executive director of the Tabas Hotel.

Jo Ann Tabas worked as a waitress in the Downingtown Inn's dining room, manned the hotel's reservation desk and later was the sales manager of the Twelve Caesars.

The youngest Tabas, daughter Susan, pitched in, too, with a variety of jobs. She parlayed her interest in horseback riding by encouraging her father to build a twenty stall barn to house horses for the resort's trail riding activity. Susan frequently accompanied guests on their rides.

Extended family found work there, too. As a seventeen year-old pianist, nephew Jimmy Roberts, now a Broadway composer, cut his teeth professionally by entertaining guests in the Inn's lounge and nightclub, while nephew Peter Koeppel worked there, too, manning the pro shop at the golf course.

"In the hospitality business, greetings are important," Dan would say. "When one of our kids greeted a guest and introduced themselves as a member of the Tabas family, people were very impressed."

For more than seventeen years, the Downingtown Inn Golf & Tennis Resort attracted guests from around the world. Thanks to Dan Tabas, they poured hundreds of millions of dollars into the Chester County economy and put it on the map, making it possible for thousands of local residents to find meaningful work at decent wages. One of them was Joe Campbell.

"Dan gave an awful lot of people an opportunity. He was an excellent motivator who knew how to get the most out of people, and he was smart enough to let people do the day-to-day administration while he passed his vision along and shaped the venture, whether it was a building, a hotel, a dinner theater or a bank."

But Dan also knew that nothing lasted forever, Campbell said, which is why in 1972 the Tabases accepted an offer they couldn't refuse. It came from the Ramada Hotel organization, which proposed a merger. In a deal that involved millions of dollars in cash and stock, the Tabas brothers became Ramada's largest stock holders, and

DANIEL TABAS

they took seats on the giant resort chain's board of directors. As part of the deal, Dan and Evelyn stayed on to manage the Inn and act as its official host and hostess. Mickey Rooney stayed on, too.

While 1972 was a milestone year as far as their business interests were concerned, it was also a year of great sadness for the Tabas family. On July 17 the man Dan admired most, his beloved father, Samuel "Pop-Pop" Tabas, passed away at age eighty-seven after a long illness. He was laid to rest in the Roosevelt Memorial Park in Trevose, Pennsylvania.

"My father was a great man," Dan would say. "He came to this country with little more than the shirt on his back and a dream. He overcame setbacks and tragedies that could have destroyed him, but he had a vision, which is why he named his business Acorn Iron and Supply. He always said, 'From a little acorn a giant tree can grow. Boy, was he right." Samuel Tabas's obituary appeared in the *Philadelphia Bulletin*:

> *Samuel Tabas, a retired real estate developer and steel contractor, died yesterday at Hahnemann Hospital. He was 87 and lived at 2401 Pennsylvania Avenue. He was also founder of the Samuel Tabas Family Foundation, a philanthropic trust. In 1904 Mr. Tabas founded Acorn Iron and Supply Company. He retired in 1960 as the firm's chairman. He and sons Charles and Daniel started Downingtown Industrial Enterprises, an industrial and recreational development in Downingtown. It now includes the Downingtown Motor Inn, industrial plants and retail establishments. Mr. Tabas was on the board of governors of Temple Adath Israel of the Main Line. He was a trustee of the Jewish National Fund and Beth Jacob schools. He is survived by his wife Ida and his two sons.*

In remembrance, Dan donated fifteen acres in Downingtown for a park which will forever bear his fathers' name — the Samuel Tabas Memorial Park. Dan also purchased one hundred plots at the memorial park for family members and their descendants.

New Ventures

Also in 1972, Dan launched the Riverfront Restaurant and Dinner Theatre in Philadelphia. It could seat five-hundred-twenty guests and would stage hundreds of performances a year. At the same time, he continued to oversee the operations of the Downingtown Inn under the Ramada

A Pasture Becomes a Gold Mine

Aerial view of the new Tabas Hotel opened in 1981 directly across the street from the original Downingtown Inn

umbrella, but the corporate culture was too stifling for an innovative and resourceful entrepreneur like Dan Tabas.

"He hated the corporate bureaucracy," Joe Campbell said, so in 1975, Dan left to strike out once again on his own. Over the next five years, he greatly expanded the Tabas family's business interests. He turned his attention to the Philadelphia riverfront where he added to the dinner theater by building and launching the Riverfront Complex, which included the Riverfront Restaurant and the posh Admiral's Club, a private gourmet dining facility on the Delaware at Poplar Street.

The next year he purchased a former Ford showroom on City Line Avenue at Belmont Drive, also in Philadelphia. Dan transformed it into a magnificent dinner theater, the City Line Dinner Theater, and the Twelve Caesars banquet facility.

As busy as he was, Dan agreed to serve on the board of directors of the Bank of Old York Road. It wasn't Dan's first exposure to a bank's boardroom. In 1957, he was elected a director of the Industrial Valley Bank and served on its board for 25 years as well as on the board of the Industrial Valley Title Insurance Company. He served as president of the Jewish National Fund from 1975 through 1976. In 1980, Dan acquired the controlling interest in the Bank of King of Prussia, which was renamed Royal Bank of Pennsylvania with Dan as its chairman and chief executive officer.

Philadelphia real estate developer Ed Tepper, president of Tepper Properties, Inc., was one of the businessmen Dan invited to invest in his newest venture, the Bank of King of Prussia. Ed didn't hesitate. He confidently invested one hundred thousand dollars. "I never doubted that it would make money," Ed remembered.

Ed had known Dan Tabas for many years. His father had been the Tabas family doctor and was also a close family friend. Ed was well aware of the Tabas family's work ethic, and he was confident that Dan "knew how to attract and keep customers for the bank."

One way he did it was by taking them on annual all-expense-paid cruises. Dan and Evelyn chartered entire ships and hosted employees, friends, and suppliers, as well as family members and bank customers. They loved being the host and hostess, and it gave them great pleasure to see their guests enjoying themselves. "It was the only time my father could really relax," said Susan Tabas Tepper.

The Tabas brothers missed the hotel business, but they passed on several opportunities to buy the Downingtown Inn back from Ramada. When their no compete agreement with Ramada expired — the Tabas brothers had been prohibited from owning a hotel within five hundred miles of Downingtown — Dan built a new resort hotel, the Tabas Hotel, on the north side of Route 30, directly across the road from the Downingtown Inn.

The three story, three hundred-room hotel and resort opened its doors on March 16, 1981, the very day the no compete clause expired. Advertisements and brochures trumped the news:

MICKEY ROONEY & DAN TABAS TOGETHER AGAIN AT THE MAGNIFICENT TABAS HOTEL

Mickey Rooney himself cut the ribbon, and a giant caricature of the Hollywood star adorned an outside front wall. Not long

A Pasture Becomes a Gold Mine

Mickey Rooney cuts the ribbon officially opening the Tabas Hotel while Dan and Evelyn, and Charles Tabas, look on

after the Tabases launched their new hotel, Ramada sold the Downingtown Inn, which became the Best Western Brandywine Inn and Resort.

Among the amenities of the Tabas Hotel were sumptuous ballrooms with magnificent crystal chandeliers, luxuriously decorated rooms and suites, indoor and outdoor swimming pools, a gymnasium, saunas, Jacuzzis, and a large gazebo. A bowling alley — the Tabas-built and owned Bowling Palace — was next door.

Let There Be Shows

The state-of-the-art facility could accommodate six hundred guests for banquets and dinners, but it wasn't supposed to be a resort hotel, at least not at first. However, when people heard that the Tabases had opened a new hotel in Downingtown, "they came looking for the food, the shows and the entertainment," said Linda Tabas Stempel, its executive director.

Linda was the hostess, scheduled the activities, and even took guests on guided tours of Downingtown in one of Dan's limousines. She also conducted tours of the Tabas Hotel's huge kitchen every afternoon at five o'clock, hosted the Friday evening cocktail party, and taught aerobics classes. But guests also wanted entertainment, so Dan said, "Let's have shows."

Linda began booking acts for the hotel's nightclub, the magnificent Las Vegas style Starlight Room, which featured superstar entertainers like singers Tony Martin, and comedians Freddie Roman and Pat Cooper.

A view of the Ben Franklin bridge from the Riverfront Restaurant and Dinner Theater. This waterfront version of Daniel's Restaurant was duplicated at the Tabas Hotel in Downingtown, featuring similar gourmet fare.

A Pasture Becomes a Gold Mine

Looking back on his career in the hospitality business, Dan said:

When we operated the Downingtown Inn and Golf Club, in Downingtown, we had a building that we had built out of an old barn that was there. It really became beautiful and seated about 300 people for dinner. It had its own kitchen. We had some bedrooms above. It was really nice, set out right on the golf course. We had a very good theater producer who brought us real Broadway shows like Annie Get Your Gun, My Fair Lady, The King and I *and* Showboat. *We charged $12.95 for the show and the meal. Drinks were extra. And that caught on very well. We had many nights full capacity. On Saturday we ran a show in the evening and a matinee. The same thing on Sunday, and two shows on Wednesday. The hotel was a big success. The golf course was a big success. The dining room was a big success. It was just overwhelming, the kind of business we did there and the money we made.*

Then we had the Riverfront Restaurant and Dinner Theater, which overlooked the Delaware River. It became very popular. It seated five hundred people and it had great success, too. Then we opened another dinner theater, which became a catering facility with big banquet halls on City Line Avenue called Twelve Caesars. It seated six hundred people. All in all, it was great fun and I'm sorry we don't have dinner theaters now.

■ DANIEL TABAS

HEADLINERS WHO APPEARED AT THE D

Left: Band leader Cab Calloway

Below: Singer Bobby Rydell

Above: Comedian Henny Youngman

Right: Tony and Oscar nominee Peggy Cass

A Pasture Becomes a Gold Mine

vningtown Inn and the Tabas Hotel

Left: Funnymen Frank Ford and Jackie Mason

Below: Singer Robert Goulet

Above: Laugh-In Stars Dan Rowan and Dick Martin

Right: Comedian Charlie Callas

DANIEL TABAS

Comedian Corbett Monica

Actor and comedian Dick Shawn

Actor and comedian Morey Amsterdam

Cinque Della Notte

A Pasture Becomes a Gold Mine

Clockwise from top: TV's George Jessel, Comedian Jack Carter, Tony winner Anna Maria Alberghetti, Metropolitan Opera star Jan Peerce, Movie Star Lana Turner

DANIEL TABAS

Above: Singer Rudy Valley

Singer and actor Theodore Bikel

A Pasture Becomes a Gold Mine

Right: The Tabases and Tony Bennett

Left: Hello Dolly's Carol Channing

Right: TV's Mike Douglas and John Raitt

DANIEL TABAS

Mickey Rooney, Dan Tabas and Trudy Haynes

A Pasture Becomes a Gold Mine

Above: Sergio Franchi and Pat Cooper

Dan with Elke Sommer

The whole world steps aside for the man who knows where he is going
Unknown

THE LOAN RANGER

Dan had a unique gift – he could see the reward behind the risk, and he believed that he could do anything if he worked hard enough.
Jim McSwiggan

In the 1980s, Dan Tabas donned a new hat — a white Stetson to become the Loan Ranger.

The eighties brought sweeping changes to America, among them the introduction of the personal computer and, with the election of Ronald Regan to the White House, the loosening of government regulation of many industries, including the banking industry. Dan had been intrigued by the banking business ever since the 1930s, when hundreds of banks collapsed in the greatest economic calamity the world had ever seen, the Great Depression. His father's savings vanished overnight. Young Dan's childhood savings were wiped out, too – he lost the fourteen dollars he had painstakingly saved by depositing one nickel every week in his school bank account. While that experience made him wary of bankers, it was also the catalyst that sparked a life-long interest in the business of banking, which he learned up close and first-hand as a director of the Industrial Valley Bank and later as a director of the Bank of Old York Road.

In 1980, Dan acquired the Bank of King of Prussia which became the Royal Bank of Pennsylvania. Today, thanks to Dan's vision, it is known as Royal Bank America.

A 1984 *Forbes* article praised Dan for his leadership of Royal Bank of Pennsylvania, and found the bank to be "exceptionally profitable." Said Forbes, "Net income has risen fivefold since the Tabases took over," while "per-share earnings almost trebled to $1.23 from 42 cents." The secret to the bank's success was its "exploiting a neglected market – smaller business and professional borrowers of $25,000 to $950,000."

From Hospitality to Banking

"We brought our experience in the hospitality industry to the banking business," said Lee Tabas, who would work alongside his father as Royal's president. "We emphasized customer care, and we were among the very first banks to offer Saturday banking hours."

DANIEL TABAS

Dan, center, with sons Robert, left, and Lee, right

The Loan Ranger

Dan, Jo Ann, Lee, Linda and Evelyn at sign announcing the opening of Royal Bank headquarters in Narberth, 1981

The Philadelphia Inquirer of June 21, 1988, noted Royal's success. Its headline read:

AMID THE GIANTS, ROYAL BANK FINDS PROFITABLE OPERATING ROOM

While the big banks have been getting bigger...smaller banks and savings institutions have found there is still plenty of room to maneuver. And quite profitably, thank you!

Royal Bank of Pennsylvania...based in Narberth, placed first on the list [of publicly held bank and thrift institutions in the eight county area around Philadelphia], with a return on average assets [ROA] of 2.72 percent, far higher than the area's other publicly traded financial institutions.

In little more than eight years, Royal Bank of Pennsylvania had grown from one office and thirty-five employees in

Above: Royal Bank of Pennsylvania board of directors visits the United States Mint, Philadelphia, 1986

1980 to eight offices and eighty employees in 1988, and had outperformed the area's banking giants.

"Smaller banks, such as Royal, tend to perform better than large banks in ROA rankings because they typically have more capital, or net worth, proportionate to their assets," the *Inquirer* declared. "CoreStates, for example, had a 1987 return on assets of 1.10 percent, considered excellent for such a big bank but only good enough for eighth place in the rankings for the Philadelphia area."

And, the newspaper declared, "Royal's profit performance...was as notable as the ten gallon hats the bank's officers have been known to wear in their advertising, in which they call themselves, 'The Loan Rangers.'"

The idea for the innovative ad campaign was Dan's. It was sparked when a bank customer rode a horse into a drive-in

The Loan Ranger

The Lone Ranger visits the Loan Ranger

Dan Tabas, left, with Joe Campbell inside Joe's office at Royal Bank headquarters, Narberth

branch to make a deposit.

Said Dan, "We decided to become the Loan Rangers, a take-off on the Lone Ranger," the 1930s radio drama which Dan had spent hours listening to as a youngster, and which his sons watched on television in the 1950s and 1960s. Dan appeared on billboards and in advertisements as the Loan Ranger, and the bank gave away ten gallon hats and key chains – tiny toy guns in leather holsters. It was a daring promotion. Nothing like it had been seen before in the staid banking industry, but it worked.

"It got us attention, and that's what advertising is all about," Dan told the *Inquirer* reporter. Philadelphia native Betsy Z. Cohen, who founded Jefferson Bank in 1974, admired Dan's ability and

Left to right are Dan's executive assistants: Lisa Lockowitz and Diana Viglianese, pictured here with Robert, Evelyn and Dan Tabas.

Inside the Royal Bank boardroom are (left to right) Ken Tepper, Lee Tabas, Susan Tabas Tepper, Dan Tabas and Robert Tabas

said, "Dan was a brilliant banker and entrepreneur." High praise indeed for someone with her illustrious background in banking, law and real estate.

Dan wasn't a typical banker, nor was Royal Bank a typical bank; it courted customers that other larger, more traditional, banks usually avoided.

A subsequent marketing campaign garnered even more attention when Royal Bank of Pennsylvania, in yet another promotion inspired by Dan, began handing out free samples – dollar bills attached to business cards carrying photos of Dan and Lee Tabas, then-president of Royal Bank. In later years, Dan upped the ante, giving away two-dollar bills in a paper billfold that bore his photo as the Loan Ranger. "If a baker can give away cookies as samples, why can't a bank give away money?" Dan asked rhetorically.

While Royal Bank is publicly traded on the NASDAQ as Royal Bancshares under the symbol RBPAA, nearly sixty percent of the stock was, and still is, owned by the Tabas family. With Lee Tabas as the bank's president, Robert Tabas managing its Centre City offices, and Susan Tabas Tepper serving as its director of marketing, Royal Bank of Pennsylvania was, like the Downingtown Inn, Mickey Rooney's Tabas Hotel, and other Tabas enterprises, a family business.

"It gives outside shareholders great security because they know the people who are running the bank have made a hefty investment in its success," Dan explained.

"At other banks, if managers don't have a piece of the action, and if they make a mistake, they can say, 'Gee, sorry.' But people who have money on the line go out of their way to make sure they personally review every detail." And because of the family's background in the hospitality industry, "We can do what other banks can't – provide personal service," Dan said.

That dedication to personal service means always having a human being answering the phone, not a machine. It was Dan's way, and he insisted on it, which is why whenever a customer calls Royal, they always speak to a person, and if they want to speak with the bank's chairman or the president, they can.

Because of that dedication to personal service, in 2004 Royal Bank America had more than a billion dollars in assets and sixteen branches throughout Southeastern Pennsylvania and New Jersey. Two years later, Royal Asian Bank, a subsidiary, was operating five retail branches–three in the Philadelphia area and two in Fort Lee, New

Jersey, as well as a loan origination office in Annandale, Virginia to serve the Washington, D.C. market.

"Dan was a very astute businessman," says Joe Campbell, Royal's former president and CEO. "Dan encouraged us to make the bank bigger and more important." Said Robert Tabas, the bank's chairman, "Dad's vision and his techniques are instilled in each one of us."

That's because Dan Tabas was a teacher, and those who worked with him and for him were students of Tabas University. He taught them the art of negotiation. Philadelphia attorney Allan Rothenberg credits Dan with teaching him how to negotiate, and counts Dan as "one of the three superstars" he has known in is life.

Dan taught his pupils that money saved was money earned. He also showed his pupils how to look at business opportunities from different angles.

"We would come up with an idea for a project and bring it to Dan, and almost always he would come up with a completely different perspective on how to make more money," said Jim McSwiggan, who began his business career as an accountant at Acorn Iron and Supply in the 1970s and rose to become the CFO of Royal Bank America. He became President of the Bank in 2009.

"Dan," Jim observed, "had a unique gift – he could see the reward behind the risk, and he believed that he could do anything if he worked hard enough," which explains how Dan could dare to create an office park in Downingtown on speculation, or how he could build a Pritikin Center at the Tabas Hotel before contacting Nathan Pritikin, its founder. Nathan Pritikin created the Pritikin Program and thereby reversed his own heart disease. At his death in 1985, the *New England Journal of Medicine* reported that Nathan Pritikin's arteries were completely free of any effects of heart disease

"Being able to make things work, to push uphill, was fun for Dan," Jim said.

"He was confident that he had the business acumen to make money." What's more, he had staying power. Scarred by the Depression and never wanting to risk home and hearth, Dan never borrowed money. Instead, he financed his projects by using his own resources or by seeking out equity partners.

While Dan was busy building Royal Bank of Pennsylvania, he was also hard at work overseeing and expanding the family's operations in the hospitality industry,

The Loan Ranger

The wedding parties joined together for a group photo

June 7, 1987: Newspapers reported the double wedding of Linda to Murray Stempel III and Susan Tabas to Ken Tepper at the Twelve Caesars. The gala was attended by 800 guests who were entertained by Lionel Hampton & His Orchestra

14 FRIDAY, JULY 31, 1987 AMERICAN-JEWISH LIFE

Sisters Linda J. Tabas And Susan K. Tabas Married in Unique Double Ceremony.

Double Wedding At Twelve Caesars

A double wedding was recently held at the Twelve Caesars, 4200 City Line Avenue, Philadelphia, PA 19131. Linda Jane Tabas was married to Murray Stempel III and her sister, Susan Kimberly Tabas, was married to Kenneth Lewis Tepper. Rabbi Fredric Kazan performed the beautiful, unique ceremony.

The brides are the daughters of Mr. and Mrs. Daniel M. Tabas of Haverford, Pennsylvania. Mr. Tabas is president of Tabas Enterprises, a part of which is the fabulous Twelve Caesars banquet facility and the Tabas Hotel in Downingtown, PA. Mr. Tabas also serves as chairman of the executive board of the Royal Bank of Pennsylvania.

Murray Stempel, III is the son of Mr. and Mrs. Murray Stempel, Jr., of Chicago, Illinois. Kenneth Tepper is the son and stepson of Mr. and Mrs. Edward B. Tepper of Villanova, PA. His mother, Debra Gross, resides in Chestnut Hill, PA.

The matron of honor for Linda Tabas was her sister, Carol Tabas (Mrs. Guy) Stofman of Haverford, PA; the best man for Murray Stempel, III was his brother, Scott Stempel, of Chevy Chase, MD.

The maid of honor for Susan Tabas was Susan Snedden of Penn Valley, PA; the best man for Kenneth Tepper was David Reape of Philadelphia, PA.

Both couples left on separate European honeymoons following the weddings and reception. About 250 guests attended pre-wedding parties and brunches at the Tabas Hotel, in Downingtown, PA; approximately 600 guests attended the ceremony and reception held at the Twelve Caesars. Lionel Hampton and his orchestra provided music at the reception along with local Fred Hall orchestra. Amongst the notable wedding guests were singer Patti LaBelle, local TV newscaster, Channel 3's Ms. Pat Ciarocchi, U.S. Deputy Attorney General Arnold I. Burns; NY radio personality Barry Farber and former mayoral primary candidate Ed Rendell.

among them the imposing Twelve Caesars banquet facility on City Line Avenue, five miles from downtown Philadelphia. It was managed by daughter Jo Ann Tabas Wurzak and son-in-law Howard Wurzak. Renowned for its lavish galas and charity functions, and for the striking statues of Roman emperors that lined its façade, the Twelve Caesars flourished. It was where Linda

Tabas married Murray Stempel III and Susan Tabas married Ken Tepper in a gala double ceremony on June 8, 1987. But it needed a nearby hotel so that its customers could house overnight guests for weddings and other functions, so Dan solved that problem by building one. Construction began next door in the fall of 1998. Two years later, on January 2, 2000, the 12-story, two-hundred-fifty room Radisson Philadelphia Hotel, opened its doors. The project raised eyebrows among many in the Philadelphia hospitality sector who saw a glut of hotel projects under construction in the area at the time, with eight thousand new hotel rooms having opened since January 1, 1998, including four thousand new hotel rooms in Center City.

The new hotel would later be refranchised and renamed the Hilton Philadelphia City Avenue. Son-in-law Howard Wurzak was the executive director and continues to be the driving force in the hotel's success. Howard met the entire Tabas family in 1982, while they were on a cruise in the Caribbean aboard the SS Norway. Howard had been involved in the hospitality industry for ten years and was vacationing after overseeing the opening of a Hilton Hotel in Albany, New York. Dan invited Howard to visit him in Philadelphia.

"I had worked for a family-owned catering and banquet business before I went to work for Hilton, so I was reluctant to become involved in another family business," Howard said. But Dan persuaded him to visit him in Philadelphia, and he was at the airport when Howard's plane arrived from Albany. Together they toured the area, and Dan showed Howard his many business interests. Two weeks later, Howard went to

Press conference for Dan's newest hotel in Philadelphia

work managing the Riverfront Dinner Theater.

"We hit it off right away," Howard recalled. "Dan was charming, unpretentious and down-to-earth."

Over the years the two men developed a special bond, and they grew especially close despite some disagreements. "We could argue on Friday, but the next day the argument was forgotten," Howard said. "He was almost always right, but he always challenged me to prove him wrong."

Howard looked upon Dan as a role model and a father figure, and he learned a lot from him about the hotel business, real estate, and investing.

Said Howard, "My father-in-law was great at investments, and at negotiating deals. I respected him and loved him, and I think about him every day."

In June 2003, Dan Tabas launched yet another project, also managed by Howard, this one next door to the Hilton City Avenue. That's when construction began on the twelve-story Homewood Suites by Hilton, Philadelphia's most luxurious extended stay facility. It opened its doors in January 2005. It was an amazing achievement, built on a ten thousand square foot piece of land overlooking the city's skyline and the Belmont Reservoir.

It was Dan's last major construction project, one that he would not live to see completed. But getting it off the ground gave him enormous satisfaction.

Then-mayor Ed Rendell, Dan Tabas and Howard Wurzak at the press conference to announce the new Hilton City Avenue in Philadelphia

Dan and Evelyn with nine of their twenty grandchildren in the gallery at Acorn Farm
Clockwise from top: Ted Tabas, Jake Wurzak, Elizabeth Tabas, Melissa Tabas, Brittany Wurzak, Alex Stempel,
Chelsea Wurzak, Jessica Stempel and Fitz Daniel Tabas Tepper

FAMILY FIRST

Many men can make a fortune, but very few can build a family
J.S. Bryan

Even though he worked from before dawn until late in the evening, Dan always found time for his family, especially his children and grandchildren. Residents in Lower Merion Township were used to to seeing the Tabas family traveling the roads in their nine-passenger limousine with Dan Tabas behind the wheel.

"Dan's entire being was devoted to his family," said Ken Tepper. "Despite his wealth and all his successes in business, his greatest satisfaction came from his own children and his grandchildren."

Every December, the young Tabas family would head south where they would stay until spring, in their winter home at 1580 Treasure Drive on Treasure Island, an area where home ownership had been restricted by covenant deeds to all but White Anglo Saxon Protestants.

Dan had been stationed in Miami Beach during World War II and had seen first hand the signs that dotted the area proclaiming "Gentiles Only" or "No Jews, No Dogs." But that didn't stop Dan and Evelyn Tabas from purchasing property where they wanted. He and Evelyn blazed the trail for Jews when they purchased their home in Haverford, and they did the same when they purchased their winter home on Miami Beach's Treasure Island.

The six Tabas children attended school there while Dan remained in Pennsylvania, overseeing the operations of Tabas Enterprises. He would fly south every weekend, usually arriving late in the evening on Friday and staying until Monday. It could be a grueling journey for him, especially in the years before jet travel, but "my father didn't want us to endure the cold Philadelphia winters," recalled Susan Tabas Tepper.

The annual winter sojourns that brought the Tabas children to the sunny south also brought them face-to-face with the ugliness of racism and segregation.

DANIEL TABAS

Evelyn Tabas outside their Treasure Island, Florida, home

1953: Ruth Brown holds Linda Tabas

That's because in 1950, Ruth Brown began doing day work at the Tabas home in Haverford. Nine months later Evelyn and Dan invited Ruth, an African-American, to join their household as a housekeeper and travel to Florida with them for the winter. She would remain with the Tabas family until she retired five decades later.

It's hard to believe today, but under the laws then in effect in Florida, the Tabases were required to build a separate entrance to their home for Ruth just because she wasn't white. The local law required her to register with the police and carry an official identification pass at all times. During one of their flights to Florida, the Tabases and Ruth were forced to land in Tampa due to inclement weather. When they tried to check into a local hotel for the night, the front desk clerk informed Dan that Ruth couldn't stay at the facility which followed a strict "White's Only" policy.

Dan wouldn't hear of it. "If she can't stay here, neither will we," he fumed, and the family, which would have taken four rooms for the night, left the hotel.

Fortunately, they were able to find other accommodations and remain together despite Florida's strict segregation laws.

Journeys Far and Wide

Dan and Evelyn almost always took their children with them when traveling abroad. "It was easier and less worrisome to take all of them with us than to give someone the responsibility of caring for them while we were away," Evelyn Tabas said. In all, the Tabases visited about fifty countries as a family. As time went on, they took to cruising. Dan would host the entire family,

Susan and Lee at the Dead Sea, Israel

The Tabas family in Venice, Italy

Evelyn, Lee and Linda with Cuban revolutionaries, Havana, 1958

extended family, close friends and key employees. "The trips were educational and fun, but most of all they helped us forge a strong family bond," said Susan Tabas Tepper. There were frequent trips to the four corners of the world with family, often bringing back people and ideas to improve the businesses, and cruises on the high seas as well as winters in Miami Beach.

Temple of Carnac, Luxor, Egypt 1978

Dan, Marilyn and Gene Koeppel, and Susan Tabas, Summer Palace, St. Petersburg, Russia, 1974

When traveling, Dan was nothing if not practical. In the years when the family would tour Europe, Dan rented a VW mini bus and all six kids piled in as they drove around the continent, stopping where and when they liked. The stops ran the gamut of a simple farm stand for fresh fruit, bread and cheese, to the finest 4 star restaurant so Dan could get ideas for his menus back home.

As the family grew, cruising as a means of travel became one of the more preferred modes of travel.

"I remember one day when Dad was totally fed up with the huge quantity of luggage we had - daughters and daughters-in-law, plus babies can generate a lot - I think the bellman counted 28 pieces, and that's when he said the next trip would be a cruise," recalled Susan Tabas Tepper.

Dan and Evelyn became enamored with cruising, Dan more so not only because he relinquished responsibility for the massive amount of luggage, but it was an efficient way to have an all-inclusive vacation. He and Evelyn also liked that the family would come together every evening, no matter what adventures they enjoyed separately during the day.

Family cruise, 1997, twenty-two of the then thirty-one member Tabas clan pictured

Evelyn and the six Tabas children in Miami Beach on their first yacht, "1796 House," named for the restaurant at the Downingtown Inn & Golf Club

Dan often used the term, "busman's holiday," for the family trips incorporating hotel stays, emphasizing the concept of how difficult it was to avoid the temptation of working while on vacation with the children. He was always looking for new ideas and employees for his hospitality based businesses. One of the ways Dan avoided this, much to Evelyn's delight, was to buy a place in an area of the country they loved.

Always looking for a good deal, Dan killed two birds with one stone; the ownership of real estate had proven to be a good investment and as the family grew, all those hotel rooms were a small fortune. Among the family vacation residences are; "Desert Island," Rancho Mirage, California; "Deere Run," Quechee, Vermont; "Mystic Pointe," Aventura, Florida, "Old Port Cove," North Palm Beach, Florida and the place whose construction was the culmination of Dan's dream to recapture his childhood home in Atlantic City, the sprawling "Acorn by the Sea," in Ventnor, New Jersey.

Family First

Acorn-by-the-Sea, easterly view from the beach, Ventnor, New Jersey

During the Depression, when Sam Tabas lost the family home on Massachusetts Avenue right after young Daniel's Bar Mitzvah, Dan always dreamed of owning land once again on Absecon Island. Dan, in collaboration with architect Jack Swerman, a second cousin who assisted him on previous projects, began construction on Acorn-by-the-Sea in 1998. The mammoth structure was completed in 2000. With the gated entrance on Marion Avenue and the exit on Baton Rouge, the beach house extends a full city block on the boardwalk, with seventeen bedrooms to house all the children, their spouses and the growing number of grandchildren.

oying fresh Jersey corn with Zayda; (left to right) x Stofman, Greg Stofman, Alex Stempel, Fitz Tepper d Charlette in Dan's arms, Acorn-by-the-Sea

DANIEL TABAS

Evelyn with Prince Monyo sculpture of children playing, Acorn Farm

Chelsea Wurzak, Lily Stofman and Brittany Wurzak engage in a tug-of-war with a Monyo sculpture on the grounds of Acorn Farm

Dan on the front lawn of Acorn Farm with sculpture of children on a swing

Today, Dan and Evelyn Tabas' love for children can be seen in more than one hundred bronze life-size creations of children at play by the internationally acclaimed Romanian sculptor Prince Monyo Mihailescu-Nasturel. The children are suspended in motion in moments of play. They adorn Acorn Farm and the Tabas home, Acorn-by-the-Sea, on the boardwalk in Ventnor, New Jersey.

Their creator, Prince Monyo Mihailescu-Nasturel, was born into the Romanian royal family in 1926. He spent seven years in prison after the communists took power in his homeland following the Second World War. Dan, attracted by the artist's valiant fight for freedom as well as by his art, met the prince in the 1970s while he and Evelyn were strolling down Worth Avenue in Palm Beach. They noticed the flamboyant artist and his signature yellow Rolls Royce and immediately struck up a conversation about their love of classic cars. The Prince invited Dan and Evelyn to tour his nearby *Gallery Via Veneto* and the visit touched off what would become a lifelong friendship. Dan went on to become one of the sculptor's leading patrons.

Forge to honor the memory of Evelyn's father, Rabbi Sigmund J. Rome. It was a fitting tribute, highlighting the emminent Rabbi's love and respect for humanity and dedication to democracy and freedom for all. The enormous depiction of the eternal flame, especially symbolic in the Jewish religion, stands at the entrance to Valley

Evelyn and Dan with Prince Monyo at the Freedoms Foundation at Valley Forge

In 1996, Dan commissioned Prince Monyo to create a bronze, forty-eight foot rotating Eternal Flame. The Tabases generously placed this spectacular symbol of freedom at The Freedoms Foundation at Valley Forge National Park where The Freedoms Foundation is located.

Founded in 1949, The Freedoms Foundation is dedicated to celebrating the United States Constitution and the Bill of

DANIEL TABAS

Rights, and with Dan's guiding hand promulgated its own Bill of Responsibilities. Each year more than three thousand elementary and secondary school students from across the country visit the Foundation's historic campus to learn about freedom, constitutional rights, the responsibilities of citizenship and the private enterprise system. In addition, hundreds of elementary and secondary school educators participate annually in seminars and workshops on effective techniques for teaching good citizenship.

In a letter to his grandchildren, Dan wrote, "We have a lot to be optimistic about. No other economy is better… There is no better [system of] government around," which is why The Freedoms Foundation was one of Dan Tabas' favorite philanthropies. He devoted many hours to it. Not only did he serve on its board for many years — he was first elected in 1982 — he served as

Eternal Flame *installation, Freedoms Foundation headquarters, Valley Forge National Park*

Right, dedication plaque on base of sculpture

its chairman from 2000 to 2002.

"The Freedoms Foundation was very important to my father," Dan's daughter Linda Tabas Stempel said. "He believed that it is vitally important to the future of our nation to teach young people about free enterprise, American capitalism and liberty."

Philadelphia news anchor Pat Ciarrocchi was on The Freedoms Foundation board with Dan. "At it's most critical time, he saved The Freedoms Foundation," the KYW newswoman said.

The nonprofit foundation went through a difficult period in the late 1990s, but Dan "worked very hard to keep it alive," Pat remembered, putting his own money into it and tapping his extensive contacts for financial help to keep the foundation going.

Pat recalled co-signing fundraising letters with Dan, and working closely with him. Said Pat, "Dan was a rare individual. He could see a niche and pull all the forces together." What's more, "he couldn't be intimidated."

Evelyn and Dan with Gen. Norman Schwarzkopf and Philadelphia news anchor Pat Ciarrocchi. The retired commander of Operation Desert Storm and Operation Desert Shield was honored at the Freedoms Foundation for his service to Americans

Animals were an important part of Tabas family life. Acorn Farm, front lawn, 1987

While Dan loved children, he was also an animal lover. It was his custom to have the dishwashers at his restaraunts save the scraps, bringing home prime rib, steak and fish that had been left over from the hotel or the dinner theater to feed the dozens of cats and three German Shepherds; Thumper, Shep, and Heidi plus Blackie the mixed breed the children rescued and two poodles; Suki and Sammy, that lived at Acorn Farm over the years. Even though he would get home after midnight, Dan would remain outside while the felines ate to make certain that the canines didn't gobble up more than their share.

By the 1980's, Dan was already leading a frenetic life. In 1981, he took time out from his busy schedule to explain to his mother-in-law Bluma Rome in a letter why he felt he couldn't live his life differently:

> Dear Bluma,
> Your philosophies of life and your counseling to me to minimize my responsibilities are certainly well received. However, unfortunately, I've surrounded myself with abnormal responsibilities and enterprises and thus I'm having to "bear my own cross." It's very easy to counsel with lovely remarks as "take it easy" and so forth and so on, but when the facts have to be counted, there are a lot of people involved — not only guests but employees and associates that depend on teamwork to be the winning team. And having a part in directing the team strategy never allows me the right to shirk by relaxing or doing only what I want to do instead of doing what I have to do.
> I've made my own bed — I realize I am physically overextended — I don't know how to correct my problem and I hope I don't kill myself doing it. But, I have the arrogant attitude that the team must always win and thus my abnormal dedication.
> DAN

Brothers Charles and Dan Tabas beneath a portrait of their father

Tabas v. Tabas

By 1980, the Tabas family's business and their philanthropic interests were formidable, but in January 1983, Charles died at age sixty-seven. He was survived by his wife, Harriette, two sons and a daughter. Six months later, Tabas Enterprises and the City Line Dinner Theater made national headlines in June, when Dan terminated the contract of Zsa Zsa Gabor who was appearing there in the musical *Forty Carats*. The Hungarian-born starlet had demanded that theater personnel remove a group of handicapped men and women, all of whom were brain-damaged, from their front-row seats during a Thursday afternoon performance. As soon as he learned of the incident, Dan demanded that Gabor personally apologize. When she refused, saying, "I do not apologize to the king of England," Dan ordered the show's producer to fire the actress because of her "unilateral affront" to the handicapped. The incident made headlines from coast-to-coast. Dan was roundly praised by advocates for the disabled for the way he handled the incident.

Meanwhile, the harmony that had existed between Dan and his older brother didn't survive Charles' passing. In 1964, while their father Samuel was still alive, the Tabas brothers signed an agreement which stipulated that, upon the death of one of the partners, the surviving brother would be in charge of the family's enterprises. After Charles died, his heirs launched a

Dan and Evelyn hosted three generations of family, in-laws and close friends on a trip to Israel in 1997, always trying to foster close relationships within the family unit

The Tabas concept of family closeness extends to Cole Oldfield, son of longtime family nanny Jayne Oldfield, pictured here from left to right with his cousins at Stephanie Tabas' Bat Mitzvah, 2011; Cole Oldfield, Alex Stempel, Greg Stofman, Jake Wurzak and Max Stofman.

legal battle over the management of the joint businesses that would last for more than a decade, and it would drive a wedge between the once close family members.

From the time they were children, the brothers worked in the family business, but they always had different roles. "Charles was my father's right-hand man. He never had a childhood," Dan recalled. While Charles worked behind the scenes in the office, Dan did the dirty work and the deals. "I bundled old newspapers, and baled cardboard," he said. "When I was old enough, I loaded the trucks, hauled the scrap, and prepared it for shipping to the mills. I was the aggressive one, the one who negotiated the deals. Charles could have been, but he didn't choose that way."

Years after filing the lawsuit, Dan and Charles' heirs settled their differences out of court. They agreed to liquidate their jointly held properties. However, the legal wrangling heated up anew when Charles' estate sued Dan again. Once more, the parties to the litigation eventually settled the case out of court. As part of the settlement, they agreed to sell certain properties.

"They will be missed by me and many who expressed remorse at the change, but change is always for the better," Dan observed, referring to the properties. That was in April 1999. The following year, the Tabas Hotel and Downingtown Farmers Market and Auction were bought by developers. The properties, which had added so much to the region and brought joy to millions of shoppers, vacationers and conventioneers, were replaced with strip malls.

With the litigation finally behind him, Dan could once again devote all his energies to his family, his business and his civic endeavors. He wore many hats: pilot, developer, hotelier, restauranteur, banker, philanthropist, husband, father, and grandfather. At a time when most men are content to retire, Dan never stopped looking for challenges.

Dan makes a final phone call on moving out day at the Tabas Hotel; Dan relocated his offices in the Royal Plaza building, an office building he owned in Narberth

*When you reap the harvest of your land,
you shall not reap all the way to the edges of your field,
or gather the gleanings of your harvest;
you shall leave them for the poor and the stranger.*
Leviticus 23:22

A Prolific Giver

Dan, Evelyn and Robert with officials from the Jewish Federation of Greater Philadelphia cutting the ribbon to open Tabas House

Reaching out to those in need is a tradition that is deeply rooted in Judaism. In fact, giving to the poor is a duty. It is called *Tzedakah*, which is the Hebrew word for justice, kindness, and ethical behavior. *Tzedakah* is one of the three acts that can gain Jews forgiveness from sins.

The High Holiday liturgy states that God judges all who have sinned during the year, but through *teshuvah* (repentance), *tefilah* (prayer) and *tzedakah*, one can erase his or her sins.

When it came to charitable giving, Dan and Evelyn Tabas shared a simple philosophy: "Service to others should be in keeping with our own good fortune in life." Consequently, they were generous benefactors to a variety of causes, among them religious, educational, medical and patriotic organizations, and their example has been an inspiration to others.

"Every solicitation that came across his desk, Dad would look at it and would personally address his contribution," said Robert Tabas. Among their philanthropic endeavors were medical and educational

DANIEL TABAS

Hundreds of seniors are served by this complex of apartments donated by Evelyn and Dan

Dan and Evelyn break ground for a community park donated to the city of Downingtown to honor the memory of Samuel Tabas

The Samuel Tabas House provides housing for Philadelphia's seniors

institutions and both Jewish and non-Jewish causes. Projects included housing for low income senior citizens – The Daniel and Evelyn Tabas House and the Samuel Tabas House, both in Northeast Philadelphia. These apartment complexes house hundreds of older Philadelphians from all walks of life without regard to race or religion. The buildings also offer residents meals, activities and cultural events through the Jewish Federation of Greater Philadelphia and are still funded by the Tabas family.

A Prolific Giver

A day care center in Carmiel, Israel bears the Tabas family name. Dan and Evelyn and their children travelled to see the daycare center and attend the ribbon cutting. One of the grateful mothers expressed awe over the selflessness of individuals who would give to make a better life for children half way around the world they had never met.

One of the most crucial issues to the people of Israel is the lack of water during the long dry season. Dan and Evelyn donated money to build a reservoir they dedicated through the Jewish National Fund. The Tabas Reservoir serves hundreds of thousands of people.

Carol Tabas visits the Tabas Reservoir in Israel.

Above, left to right: Dan and Evelyn visit a Jewish National Fund reforestation project in Israel; the Tabases are welcomed by the Mayor of the City of Haifa, Israel

DANIEL TABAS

In 2000, Dan and Evelyn received a poignant letter from Ronald S. Lauder, the son of Estée Lauder and Joseph Lauder, founders of Estée Lauder Companies, chairman of the board of the Estee Lauder company, and the president of the Jewish National Fund:

Evelyn with Nick Randazzo, trusted financial advisor and Chief Controller of the Tabas family companies

March 15, 2000

Dear Dan and Evelyn,

It is people like you and your family who have made the work of the Jewish National Fund possible. I very much enjoyed our trip to Israel and I look forward to the dedication of the reservoir you are funding.

I am sending you this letter to welcome you to the newly formed World Chairman's Council, whose founding members are comprised of those like you who have contributed $1 million or more to the JNF over their lifetime. Beyond fundraising, I am calling upon you as a leader in the Jewish community to join me in discussion as I seek your advice on the most critical issue facing us, water, and the role it plays in bringing about peace in the Middle East. You can and will make a difference in this very vital issue.

To inaugurate the World Chairman's Council, my wife, Jo Carol, and I will be sending you an invitation in the very near future to join us for dinner at our home in New York on Tuesday, May 16th.

I hope to see you at that time, if not sooner. With all best wishes.

Sincerely,
Ronald S. Lauder
President, Jewish National Fund

Closer to home, they donated $5 million to the Wills Eye Hospital to build the Daniel and Evelyn Tabas Pavilion at Ninth and Walnut Streets in Philadelphia.

Thomas Jefferson University Hospital's Medical Respiratory Intensive Care Unit (MRICU) received a $1 million donation from Evelyn Tabas to honor Dan's memory. The gift provided needed funding to renovate the unit, which included an expanded nursing station and patient waiting room, remodeled patient rooms, and a new family and physician consultation room.

Millions more went to the Children's Hospital of Philadelphia where two of their

A Prolific Giver

Children's Hospital of Philadelphia May 2005: Three generations of the Tabas family gathered to dedicate the Evelyn and Daniel M. Tabas Cardiac Intensive Care Unit

Evelyn and Dan Tabas at CHOP

grandchildren underwent heart surgery. Carl Swansen, CHOP's director of development, worked closely with the Tabases, whose generosity endowed the hospital's cardiology reception area, the intensive care unit, and funded the creation of the Evelyn and Daniel M. Tabas Cardio Intensive Care Unit, as well as two chairs in cardiothoracic surgery: The Evelyn Rome Tabas Chair in Continuing Care and the Daniel M. Tabas Chair in Surgery. The chairs enable physician-scientists to pursue ground-breaking cardiac research and develop treatments that will save the lives of the youngest heart patients from around the world. Family support for CHOP is ongoing in grateful recognition of cancer care for another grandchild.

In 1995, Dan was given a commendation by Pitt Plastic Surgery at the University of Pittsburgh for a series of donations to enable J. William Futrell, M.D., Chief of Plastic Surgery, and his team to travel to developing countries to correct cleft palates and other birth defects for children regardless of financial ability.

And Dan and Evelyn have been generous benefactors of United Cerebral Palsy,

DANIEL TABAS

Jo Ann Wurzak, Linda Stempel, Evelyn Tabas and Lee Tabas in front of the covered entrance, United Cerebral Palsy of Philadelphia & Vicinity

where they provided funding to build a covered entrance, The Daniel M. Tabas Family Entrance Pavillion, to protect clients like their grandson Chet from the elements upon their arrival at, or departure from, the UCP's center in Philadelphia.

Thanks to a generous donation, the University of Pennsylvania created the state-of-the art Daniel M. Tabas Laboratory in Skirkanich Hall within the School of Engineering and Applied Sciences where scientists can integrate principles of physics, chemistry and mathematics with engineering concepts in order to advance medicine and health.

Lee, Linda and Robert Tabas graduated from the University of Pennsylvania. Dan wanted to do a project for the school. He met the Dean Eduardo Glandt of the

Evelyn Tabas accepts an accolade from University of Pennsylvania President Dr. Amy Gutmann and Dean Eduardo Glandt

A Prolific Giver

Robert Tabas, Lee Tabas, Evelyn Tabas and Dean Eduardo Glandt outside the Tabas Laboratory at the University of Pennsylvania's School of Engineering and Applied Sciences following the ribbon cutting in 2009

School of Engineering and Applied Science. Dan took an instant liking to the brilliant and charismatic dean, but when Dean Glandt proposed a donation to refurbish the building that held ENIAC, the world's first computer, Dan didn't think it was the right fit. "To me, a calculator is a computer." Dan teased.

Years later, after Dan's passing, Dean Glandt proposed to his family the Daniel M. Tabas Laboratory where researchers from a variety of disciplines could work together.

Another beneficiary of Dan's largesse was Hahnemann University Hospital, now affiliated with Drexel University College of Medicine, which recieved a grant for a cardiac cathaterization laboratory named for Samuel Tabas in honor of cardiologist Dr. Leonard Dreifus.

Ribbon cutting, Hahnemann Cardiac Catheterization Laboratory

Dan and Evelyn also gave generously to the Bank Street College of Education in New York City, where Evelyn did graduate work in early childhood education and on whose board she served as a trustee. Among her gifts was the Evelyn Rome Tabas and Daniel Tabas Auditorium, a state-of-the-art facility where educators and students can come together for conferences, lectures and other events..

The Haverford School in Haverford, Pennsylvania, received a generous gift from Evelyn, whose grandchildren Major Tepper, Fitz Tepper, Baron Hantig and Jason Tabas are students there. Another grandson, Jake Wurzak, was a 2004 Haverford School

Above: Evelyn cuts the ribbon to open the Evelyn R. Tabas and Daniel M. Tabas Auditorium at New York City's Bank Street College of Education, 2007

graduate. The Evelyn Tabas and Daniel M. Tabas Library honors Evelyn and the memory of her husband Dan.

Tabas grandchildren (left to right) Jason Tabas, Major Tepper, Baron Tabas Hantig and Fitz Daniel Tabas Tepper

In addition, numerous other institutions—schools, synagogues, churches (Dan was a friend of the Roman Catholic Seminary at Ireland's Maynooth College, the largest seminary in the world for Catholic priests)—health facilities and health organizations, were beneficiaries of Tabas generosity, as were individuals whose needs touched Dan and Evelyn's hearts.

One of them was Beverly Petti, a then five year-old girl who had the good fortune to share an elevator in a large Center City office building with Dan, who had been visiting an office in the building. As they rode down, Dan overheard a disturbing conversation. The man, who was obviously the father, told the crying Beverly that their family would have to split up and she would have to go into foster care. They were facing hard times and could no longer afford to stay together. When the elevator reached the lobby floor, everyone went their separate way, but Dan was upset about what he had heard. It gnawed at him. He couldn't sleep that night thinking of the little girl's plight. He vowed to help the family. But how would he find them?

He and Evelyn decided to print flyers that described the father and daughter and asked for information about them. Dan dispatched son Robert and son-in-law Howard Wurzak to the building to do a floor-by-floor canvass and leave the flyers at each of the offices. At first, workers in the building were suspicious of the intentions of those passing out the flyers, but within a few days a lawyer in the building contacted them. That's when Dan learned the identity of the father and daughter, and of their circumstances. He and Evelyn became their bene-

Beverly Petti

factors, and the Tabas family remains close to Beverly, now a grown woman with children of her own, to this day.

"There were many more similar incidents over the years, but Dan kept them to himself," said Louise Golden, his longtime executive assistant. "He had a side to him that many of his business associates were unaware of — he was a softie when it came to children and the elderly."

"My father was inundated with charitable requests, but as busy as he was, he opened every one," noted Susan Tabas Tepper.

Money wasn't all that Dan gave generously. He was also generous with his time, talent and expertise. Among the organizations that benefited from his service were the Freedoms Foundation at Valley Forge, which he served as chairman of the board; the Tabas Family Circle, which he served as president; the Jewish National Fund — Philadelphia Council, which he served as president and chairman of the board; the Children's Hospital of Philadelphia's Children's Circle of Care, and the American Interfaith Institute.

Dan and Evelyn in Israel meeting with Prime Minister Benjamin Netanyahu

Another very special commitment from Dan, following a request by personal phone call from Israeli Prime Minister Benjamin Netanyahu, was finalized on July 14, 2004, when a jumbo jet with four hundred men, women and children from thirty-

A Prolific Giver

three U.S. States and four Canadian provinces landed at Israel's Ben Gurion Airport. Emblazoned on the outside of the airplane, just below the pilot's window, was the name "Daniel M. Tabas." The plane took off from New York's John F. Kennedy Airport the day before. The flight had been organized by Nefesh B'Nefesh, which in Hebrew means "soul to soul." Through donations, Nefesh B'Nefesh provides financial aid and support to Americans and Canadians interested in "making aliyah" – emigrating – to Israel. The flight that brought the new settlers that day was made possible by a gift from Dan and Evelyn. A second Nefesh B'Nefesh flight the following year, also supported by Evelyn in honor of Dan, brought hundreds more settlers to Israel.

The family tradition of philanthropy instilled by Evelyn and Dan continues through their children and grandchildren.

Tabas family members at JFK. Top photo, left to right: Major Tepper, Dagny Tepper, Lee Tabas, Evelyn Tabas, Jo Ann Wurzak, Carol Tabas

Clockwise: Carol Tabas; the Boeing 747 named The Daniel M. Tabas Aliyah Flight; *Evelyn and Carol stand next to the jet way*

A thing of beauty is a joy forever
John Keats

Patron of the Arts Collector of Classics

It may seem paradoxical that a man who cut his teeth in the rough and tumble world of scrap iron would one day become a connoisseur of fine art, but with Dan Tabas there was no paradox. He had an eye for splendor. For example, he saw beauty in a pile of rubble that was once a brass works and created a thriving industrial park from the fieldstone. From an empty field in Downingtown he created a beautiful resort that was renowned the world over. And together he and Evelyn built one of the most impressive private collections of objects d'art anywhere – more than two thousand pieces from around the world.

They were collected at galleries in Paris, London, New York, Palm Beach, China and Egypt, and at Christies and Sothebys – oil paintings, Judaica, as well as statuary, silver artifacts, antique furniture and unique crystal pieces. Dan and Evelyn purchased items that appealed to them for aesthetic reasons, hardly ever for their perceived future value.

Field Flowers, *J. Cavé, Paris 1896*

Among their first purchases was *Field Flowers,* an oil painting by the renowned nineteenth century French painter Jules Cyrillic Cavé. Dan and Evelyn spotted the painting in the window of an art gallery on Lincoln Road in Miami Beach. They were struck by how much it looked like their daughter Linda, then seven years old. They debated buying what would have been one of their first major art purchases. The discussion went back and forth until Dan said, "How can we leave Linda sitting there in the window?"

Cavé was a student of Adolphe-William Bouguereau, whose tender portrayal of children appealed to Dan, who preferred the realistic style of the second half of the 19th century to the impressionist style that became popular in later decades. They reminded him of his own daughters, and of his beloved sister Frances, and he collected many Bouguereau paintings throughout the years, including "Innocence" and "L'Enfant."

The artist's life story, which in many ways mirrored his own, appealed to Dan as well. Bouguereau was a self-made man who put himself through the Ecole des Beaux-Arts by working as a bookkeeper for a wine merchant and illustrating labels for a Parisian grocer. He'd paint late into the night, creating many of his works from memory. His discipline and dedication paid off – at

Innocence (*L'innocence*), Adolphe-William Bouguereau, Paris 1893

the time of his death in 1905, Bouguereau was famous for his works and for the help he gave to young artists, like Cavé, whom he mentored.

Years later, Dan and Evelyn purchased another oil painting by Cavé, "The Budding Rose." Incredibly, the same model

Adolphe-William Bouguereau, Paris 1891

was in it, only she was several years older, and the resemblance to Linda was even more remarkable.

Léon-Bazille Perrault was another mid-nineteenth century painter whose works were favored by Dan and Evelyn. Also a student of Bouguereau – they worked side-by-side – his paintings portrayed the innocence of childhood in mythological settings. It has been said of Perrault, that "no painter of children...has more perfectly rendered the inner structure and subtle model-

The Budding Rose, J. Cavé, Paris 1903

ing of surface, the peculiar quality and graceful action of a child, in perfect physical beauty and health; and all artists know that children are the most difficult of subjects."

Like the more contemporary statues of children at play by sculptor Prince Monyo that adorn the grounds of Acorn Farm and Acorn-by-the-Sea, these works of art are testaments to Dan and Evelyn Tabas's devotion to children.

Prince Monyo blends his mechanical engineering skills into his works including his artistic creation of life-size children who appear suspended in motion in a moment of time at play in his highly acclaimed series, Children at Play, *Acorn Farm*

Patron of the Arts, Collector of Classics

Russian nesting dolls (Matryoshka), first created in Moscow in 1890, displayed in the Tabas gallery

Dan and Evelyn enjoyed collecting art on their travels. A trip to Russia in 1972 with a group of friends and family was particularly thrilling. Dan recalled:

It was an exciting trip! When we got near Russia, the pilot radioed back to the passengers that he was being diverted because he didn't use the allowable line of direction to cross over Soviet soil. When we were just five to ten miles from landing at the Moscow Airport, I saw Russian fighter planes. Our pilot nervously said, "We are going to have to fly to Helsinki, Finland. They won't allow us to land at the Moscow Airport."

This, of course, was somewhat frightening because the pilot sounded nervous talking over the plane's speaker phone.

When we finally got clearance, our plane needed fuel. We lost four hours waiting to get fuel since Pan American did not have a fueling contract at that airport. They did not extend any credit to the plane and insisted on prepayment, which after many hours was forwarded from a USA Pan American office.

We then were underway, but instead of arriving in Moscow at 2:00 p.m. that day as was scheduled, we got there about 9:00 p.m. in the dark. It was a harrowing experience.

Wherever they went, they kept an eye out for Judaica. They collected pieces from around the world—traditional items like menorahs, mezuzahs, kiddish cups and silver chalices, as well as Jewish folk art and figurines.

Classic Judaica sterling silver oil menorah representing the twelve tribes of Israel entirely made by hand.

Dan was especially fond of ornate carved silver serving pieces dating from the early 1800s to the mid-1900s, while Evelyn had a special place in her heart for antique

Ornate silver chalices and serving tray from the early 1900's, displayed in the Tabas gallery

baby carriages and dolls. While gathering objects d'art from the far corners of the world was a pastime, Dan's passion was collecting antique and classic motor vehicles.

He began in the mid 1950s with the purchase of a Model T truck. He enjoyed driving it so much he decided to search for more vehicles, eventually adding eighteen others including a 1906 Oldsmobile with a tiller instead of a steering wheel, three Rolls Royces, a custom-made Zimmer sports car, and six stretch limousines, including one made of wood with an aluminum covering. Dan's Rolls Royce Princess was built for Britain's Queen Elizabeth when she was a princess. He also found and purchased a Daimler limousine that had been used by Elizabeth after she ascended to the throne.

The vehicles did not sit idly in the garage at Acorn Farm. Dan's classic car collection was maintained by longtime Tabas employees Kenon Jenkins and Willie Hendley. "Mr. Tabas loved those cars,"

Handmade custom built cabinets display the Tabas collection of objects d'art from around the world.

Willie said. "He drove all of them." In addition to taking care of the cars and other responsibilities, Kenon and Willie were entrusted with maintaining Acorn Farm and its contents.

Dan made it a point to drive each car at least several times during the year, and neighbors around Acorn Farm were accustomed to seeing Dan behind the wheel of one of his prized vehicles, driving the highways and byways of Philadelphia's Main Line and nearby Narberth with his Loan Ranger hat atop his head.

But it wasn't only neighbors who saw Dan behind the wheel of one of his limos. Ed Tepper recalled one occasion when Dan and Evelyn, Ed and his wife and another couple went to the Spectrum where Frank Sinatra, Dean Martin and Liza Minnelli were appearing. With Dan behind the wheel of his stretch limousine, the three couples pulled into the Spectrum's parking lot and parked in an area reserved for limos. Security guards tried to prevent Dan from leaving the car, telling him that chauffeurs were required to remain with their vehicles. After some discussion and smoothing of ruffled feathers, Dan was allowed to leave his limo unattended to watch the show.

In later years, Dan finally relented and allowed himself to be driven around town by Zsolt (George) Benko who had to pass the very stringent Dan Tabas driver's test before he could get behind the wheel.

Dan with his Daimler Limousine, previously owned by Queen Elizabeth of England

He was one of a kind; irreplaceable
Linda Tabas Stempel

ONE OF A KIND

On September 12, 2003, with his family at his bedside, Dan Tabas passed away at Philadelphia's Thomas Jefferson University Hospital. Three days later, more than one thousand family members and friends filled the sanctuary at Temple Adath Israel in Merion to celebrate his remarkable life.

To Philadelphians he was the "Loan Ranger," the familiar face of Royal Bank of Pennsylvania, the real estate developer and entertainment entrepreneur who had changed the landscape and brought smiles to hundreds of thousands of men, women, and children who stayed in his hotels and enjoyed his theaters and dining facilities.

To his grandchildren he was "Zayda," the loving grandfather who would stop whatever he was doing to take their phone calls. To his children he was the hard-driving patriarch who took the Tabas family from rags to riches and left them with a legacy that will resonate throughout the region for generations to come.

To charities and civic organizations, Dan Tabas was a generous giver. Just months before his passing, he took a phone call from Benjamin Netanyahu, former prime minister of Israel who was then serving as his country's finance minister, thanking him for the first of his several generous contributions to the Nefesh program that made it possible for hundreds of American Jews to settle in Israel.

There were moving tributes. The first was from good friend Arnold I. Burns, former Deputy Attorney General of the United States during the Reagan presidency. He told the celebrants:

Every man, woman and child in this temple has suffered a great loss with the death of Dan Tabas. That's because he positively impacted each and every one of us in one way or another.

Dan and I were good friends for over 40 years. Ours was a relationship underpinned by mutual affection and respect. Our families intertwined. For all those years we shared good times together in Salt Lake city, Washington, D.C., Philadelphia, Haverford, New York, Valley Forge, North Pole, Colorado, at the Tabas homes, during the biennial trips Dan hosted for friends and customers to Bermuda and to Caribbean ports, at our home in Westhampton Beach, among many other places.

President Ronald Reagan and First Lady Nancy Reagan greet Dan and Evelyn in the White House

To me, Dan was the quintessential Renaissance man. He was an innkeeper. A hotel keeper. A restaurateur. A banker and a builder. He mastered his own ship, piloted his own plane, drove his own Winnebago, kept horses, collected paintings and objects d'art. He put together his own museum, collected automobiles, collected and ran homes east, west, north and south, and he collected good people, so many of whom are in the temple today.

He was a master of so many subjects. One and only one example: He was a lox maven without peer. He knew all there was to know about Scottish salmon, Norwegian salmon, Alaskan salmon, Atlantic salmon, Nova Scotia salmon -- even belly lox. I suspect that, like Will Rogers, he never met a lox he didn't like.

Through the years, I always said if I ever had a difficult problem to solve, Dan Tabas was the man I would consult — whether it was construction, purchasing anything from a piano to a car to a home, business, commerce, politics or even law, my own field. He was wise. He accumulated a great deal of wisdom.

And, Dan was generous. He was forthcoming in tangible ways and had enormous generosity of spirit. He and Evelyn have given a small fortune to worthy charitable endeavors.

And he never forgot his humble beginnings, notwithstanding his uncanny knack for creating wealth. He had the touch of a Midas in his business dealings. He knew he was "Mulke's" son. That's why, I am convinced, he filled his own gas tank. I never saw him in a "full serve" section of a filling station.

We are always saddened at the loss of a loved one, or a good friend or a solid pillar of our community. But I must confess I feel sadder — saddest — when we lose a strong person, a charismatic personality, a person larger than life, that's because the void left behind is so much greater. Yes, Dan was a special man - a oner.

He was also a great communicator. He always found time in a crushing schedule to send written communications — about family, current events, Jewish issues, and the successes of others — to his inner circle. Not a week went by that I did not hear from him.

Dan has left behind a great legacy for all of us, but especially for his children, Lee, Linda, Jo Ann, Carol, Robert and Susan, and especially for his grandchildren, too numerous for me to name individually. But each one of you

President George H.W. Bush

Senator Ted Kennedy

grandchildren is a precious link in the Tabas family history. Yes, Dan and Evelyn raised a fine family.

As long as we live, Dan, you will live on with all of us, you enriched our lives, and we will not forget you.

He was followed to the podium by another good friend, Memphis real estate developer Jack Belz.

We are gathered here today with great sadness and with heavy hearts. It was not many weeks ago that my wife, Marilyn, and I made airline reservations to come to Philadelphia from Memphis to celebrate Dan's special 80th birthday event. It was on the very next day we were advised that Danny was in the intensive care area and, of course, the birthday celebration had to be postponed. We all felt that it would simply be delayed, and we would later enjoy an even more splendid affair.

Marilyn and I first met the Tabases just a bit more than twenty-five years ago at the wedding of our daughter, Jan, to Andy Groveman. We immediately found that we had many common *interests and our friendship grew quickly and strong, and we shared many wonderful occasions together.*

Dan, as everyone knows, truly did things on a grand scale. This is clearly illustrated by the six different residences which he and Evelyn have, stretching from literally the West Coast to the Northeast areas of our country, and, as well, by the extensive collection of stretch limousines in which he had so much pride and enjoyment; and not being satisfied to take guests out on a small yacht, but rather to entertain on a chartered cruise ship which could accommodate hundreds of relatives and friends. These are some of the qualities of our Dan Tabas, which were truly unique to him.

It is hard to know how to speak for just a few minutes about Dan Tabas.

He was truly a giant of a man. He was certainly a brilliant businessman, entrepreneur and a visionary, a man whose advice and counsel were sought after by an enormous number of people for a myriad of subjects. He had a phenomenal business instinct. We could quickly develop a huge list of illustrations. Very prominent among them is the Royal Bank of Pennsylvania, which he literally grew and expanded one hundred-fold, and made it one of the most statistically profitable banks in the United States. He had that sixth sense as to real estate, to select locations many, many years before they would reach their greatest potential. In fact, he was the epitome of that saying in the real estate industry that the three key essentials are location, location, location.

President Gerald Ford

DANIEL TABAS

Dan's accomplishments and contributions to the economy and welfare of the Downingtown area were vast and impressive, as was his establishing the Exton Industrial Park. His activities and accomplishments on the riverfront, including Acorn Iron, which he grew into a mighty live oak, and at Twelve Caesars, were memorable and brought much pleasure to thousands of people per year, as did his hotel resorts in Downingtown. All of these hotels, clubs and restaurant facilities, including the beautiful City Line Hilton Hotel, were another means of entertaining and serving countless thousands of family, friends and the business community.

Dan Tabas was an extremely generous man, both with his time and in

United States Secretary of Homeland Security, then-governor Tom Ridge

One of a Kind

United States Senator Robert Dole

the material sense. He and Evelyn contributed graciously, generously and energetically to a vast number of very significant causes and institutions, including hospitals, educational institutions, housing for the elderly, the Jewish National Fund, and other Jewish and general causes.

He was a true role model and a man of enormous enthusiasm and, in my opinion, among the greatest of communicators. He enjoyed writing letters and receiving letters from and about friends and family. He truly kept up to date on literally all topics. He was a prolific writer who loved to share copies of his correspondence with special family and friends. It seems that he never failed to take note of a newspaper article of import, and never failed to write a congratulatory note or letter to every one of his friends and family about whom he would learn something of note. I considered myself very privileged to have been on a certain list that regularly received copies

DANIEL TABAS

Donald Trump

of correspondence he had with friends and acquaintances from all walks of life, and from all places on the globe.

I will miss this privilege. Dan demanded perfection from all of his associates, and that was the standard that he set for himself in everything that he did.

Dan was a proud man, an avid collector of art, and of memorabilia. A visit to his office not only revealed his love of art, but also was a history lesson of his and his family's life by looking at the pictures which covered every square inch of the wall surfaces.

Dan and I shared a love of art, and many times acquired identical pieces by Prince Monyo, a sculptor friend of

Dan and Donald, both one of a kind "jewels," found a unique friendship in their mutual admiration and respect for each other

ours in Palm Beach. We each had perhaps 100 or more of his sculptures, and placed them not only in personal residential surroundings, but also in commercial and institutional buildings and in landscaped areas, such as the huge Eternal Flame sculpture which he was so proud of, and placed at the Freedoms Foundation at Valley Forge, to help bring pride and joy to the many people who view them during a special visit or casually passing by.

Dan was proud of his parents, his grandparents, his family, and proud, and rightfully so, of what he had been able to accomplish with his life-partner, Evelyn, and through his unlimited energy and brilliance during his long and intensive work life.

I can remember many times receiving a copy of memoranda that he had written to his children expressing his feelings about a certain thing, or giving them some facts concerning their heritage and their family that they may not have been quite as aware of as he felt they should be.

Dan was very proud of his six children, and took special delight in his grandchildren. Nothing gave him more pleasure than to describe what they were doing in their own personal activities and in their roles in the Tabas family accomplishments and commitments.

I never dreamed that I would be here in Philadelphia on Monday, September 15, to express my feelings in this type of a sad and mournful time. Dan and Evelyn Tabas were a fantastic partnership. They were very easy to know and to love. My wife, Marilyn joins with me, as does the entire Belz family from Memphis, in

Pennsylvania Governor Ed Rendell

Back Row: Howard Wurzak, Robert Tabas, Dr. Janine Tabas, Prime Minister Margaret Thatcher, Dan Tabas, Ken Tepper
Front Row: Susan Tabas Tepper, JoAnn Wurzak, Evelyn Tabas

expressing our tremendous sorrow at the enormous loss that we are all sharing as we approach the days of awe and judgment. It is our family's sincere hope and prayer that you will find strength and the resolve to continue his unique legacy.

Jack was followed to the podium by the Tabas children – Lee, Linda, Jo Ann, Carol, Robert and Susan. With her brothers and sisters at her side, Linda delivered the tribute.

Friends and family, thank you for being here today to honor our father, Daniel Tabas, It wasn't easy to be ambivalent about our Dad. I don't recall ever hearing anyone say, "Dan Tabas, what a nice man!" People who dealt with him in business negotiations may have called him a blankety-blank. But mostly I heard people say, "Dan Tabas - what an incredible man!"

My Dad had many facets, like an intricately cut diamond — brilliant, fiery, rare. Those of you who knew him well saw beyond the surface into his complex interior and marveled at the softness of the heart within.

One of a Kind

Ambassador Walter Annenberg, Mrs. Leonore Annenberg and U.S. Deputy Attorney General Arnold I. Burns

DANIEL TABAS

Larry King

If you wanted to imagine what it was like to be in his shoes or what it was that made him tick, you might try a few of these things:

Donate a couple of million dollars to a hospital or your favorite charity, and on the way home from the dedication ceremony drive five miles out of the way to get the gas that's 2 cents a gallon cheaper.

Get a perfectly ripe pear, Dad's favorite fruit, slice it, and enjoy it with your child, always being sure that they get the last delicious piece.

Hire a few 18-year-olds with good smiles and firm handshakes to work in your restaurant or hotel. Give them your guidance, your wisdom, and your trust, then watch them go on to become the president of a bank, a senior pilot for Delta, or a major real estate developer in Philadelphia.

To imagine what it's like to have walked in Dad's shoes, buy a dozen pairs of genuine leather-like shoes from the Haband catalog because they're only $19.99 each, and convince yourself that they're comfortable because the price was so good.

At age 75, when you really should relax, build a 17-bedroom home at the shore so all your children and grandchildren can visit. While you're at it, you may as well build a 250-room hotel.

Read an article that's interesting and have your assistant photocopy it and mail it to 100 people with your comments.

Open every piece of junk mail that most people would discard because there might be a plea from a charity that will touch your heart.

Be impatient while you're talking on the speakerphone and need an intelligent answer from someone immediately. Then, on the next phone call, pretend like you have all the time in the world when a grandchild is telling you about their day at school.

Go to the senior citizen two dollar movie matinee. Next, get the seven dollar hair cut from your Narberth barber then go back to your office and arrange to charter an entire cruise ship for your best customers and friends.

Fly in private jets with Donald Trump and Ronald Lauder. Stroll down the corridors of the Federal Reserve Bank. Sip tea in the White House. Really, really enjoy the chicken sandwich at Wendy's in the companionship of your groundskeeper who has

Bill Gates

Dan and Evelyn with Jimmy Carter

been with you for 40 years.

Marry a warm, sensitive, educated spouse who will be at your side and smooth over all those feathers you've ruffled along the way. For fifty-four years, build a life full of love and compassion that includes six children and twenty grandchildren, each full of their own unique talents and passions.

Hug your children tightly, set a good example. Be a mentor, irritate, agitate, mediate. Be relentless. Inspire them. Adore them. Tell them that you love them. Then maybe you can imagine what it was like to be our Dad. No one can fill his shoes for us.

He was one of a kind, irreplaceable. We will all miss him greatly. Each of us, his children, grandchildren, and all of those whose lives he touched, even in the smallest way, will carry part of him within us forever.

Tributes poured in from luminaries and civic leaders. Donald Trump wrote, "He was an amazing man and a good friend, and even though he was quite ill in recent years, I thought he would be around forever."

Philadelphia Mayor John Street wrote, "He was a credit to his synagogue, the community, and indeed this City. His contributions are immeasurable and stand as a tribute to his effectiveness and a testimony to his memory."

Montgomery County District Court Judge Henry J. Schireson wrote that he was "so moved at Dan's service on Monday to see your beautiful family and the enormous grace and dignity with which you comported yourselves. Perhaps this was the ultimate tribute to a man who valued family above all else."

The jurist, who had known Dan for many years, summed up the spirit and soul of this remarkable man: "He had a fierce will to succeed and the force of personality to win people over to his side... he could be tough, [but] he was also kind and generous. Dan obviously enjoyed people, and his spirit was contagious."

"He was a true giant," wrote Pennsylvania Governor Ed Rendell. "A leader of one of Philadelphia's greatest and most influential families." An "incredible,

Dan with Frank Rizzo, Norman Zarwin, and Col. Eli Schwartz, Jewish National Fund award ceremony

Dan with Philadelphia Mayor Michael Nutter and Howard Wurzak

innovative, risk-taking entrepreneur — the kind who built our city and our state. Through his energy and focus, thousands of jobs were created helping families build better lives and better futures. Dan's charitable endeavors were nothing short of legendary, having the effect of giving some of our society's most vulnerable people real opportunity."

From Saint Patrick's College, Maynooth, Ireland's National Seminary & Pontifical University in County Kildare, Ireland, Monsignor Dermot Farrell wrote to Evelyn Tabas:

Dear Evelyn,

On behalf of all of us, His Eminence, Cardinal Desmond Connell, Archbishop Sean Brady, their two brother Archbishops and the thirteen Bishops who comprise our Trustees, along with our priests, staff and seminarians, I want to extend to you, your

One of a Kind

Robert Kennedy Jr. and Ethel Kennedy

children and grandchildren, our prayers and deep sympathy on the loss of your beloved husband and our dear friend Dan. I know you, his family and the many beneficiaries of his charity, have lost a good husband, father and friend and will miss him dearly.

Dan was extraordinary. His enormous personal generosity to those less fortunate was always accompanied by his great personal respect for the value of every dollar, and he reminded us by his personal example of this principle. Dan worked very hard for everything he achieved. He never forgot his roots and never lost the common touch. His incredible acumen and monumental success as a business leader, his unswerving attention to detail and extremely hard work, were an inspiration to those of us privileged to have been numbered among his friends. Dan was never harder on anybody else than he was upon himself. He lived by noble example. His high ethical standards, his magnetic and engaging personality, his loyalty to his family and friends: his unbounded hospitality and his unabashed pride in his family and employees, were always in evidence.

In all his accomplishments, Dan's greatest friend and collaborator was

Dan and Evelyn with Ted Turner, Boys and Girls Club President's Dinner, Waldorf Astoria, New York, 2000

your noble and utterly gracious and elegant self. As you are aware, he loved you deeply and his unqualified faith in your love and character was wisely placed. In every respect you were Dan's true love, his 'valiant woman' as the psalmist wrote. It is often said that behind every great man is a great lady. Dan would be the first to assure us that this was his personal privilege and experience in his life with you.

In the end, Dan fought the good fight and finished the race with exemplary nobility and great courage. Few suffering the pain and stresses of intensive care as he did, would have fought so well and so constantly. His final struggle was heroic, as indeed was his life. We will miss his special friendship, but he remains with us in spirit, and in peace. As Sir Christopher Wren's tombstone at St. Paul's Cathedral in London states, Si moonumentum requires, circumspice (if a monument is required, just look around you). That can be stated with equal truth about the family and life work of your dearly beloved husband and best friend Dan. May he rest in peace.

The more than twelve hundred mourners who came to bid farewell to Dan Tabas arrived with heavy hearts, but they left with their spirits lifted by the tributes and eulogies they heard. For two hours, they celebrated his extraordinary life. And what a life it was! Despite early years marred by tragedy and hardship, Dan persevered, confident that he could achieve whatever he set his mind to. They heard how, as a brash young man, he spied a beautiful woman in a hotel nightclub. He vowed to his friend that he would marry her, even before he ever spoke to her. And he did. Their remarkable life together spanned fifty-four years of marriage. Evelyn, his partner in all of his endeavors, smoothed whatever feathers he ruffled, inspired their children and grandchildren, and brought out Dan's spiritual, intellectual, and compassionate sides. The mourners also heard that Dan Tabas was a man of many facets, and that he left his mark in many ways: businessman, family man, soldier, friend, mentor, role model. And as a philanthropist whose generosity touched tens of thousands at home and abroad. The Old Testament tells us that there is a time to every purpose under heaven. Among them are a time to be born, and a time to die. Dan's purpose did not end with his passing. Instead it lives on, a bright guiding light for all who will follow in his footsteps.

Old friends Mickey Rooney and Dan Tabas

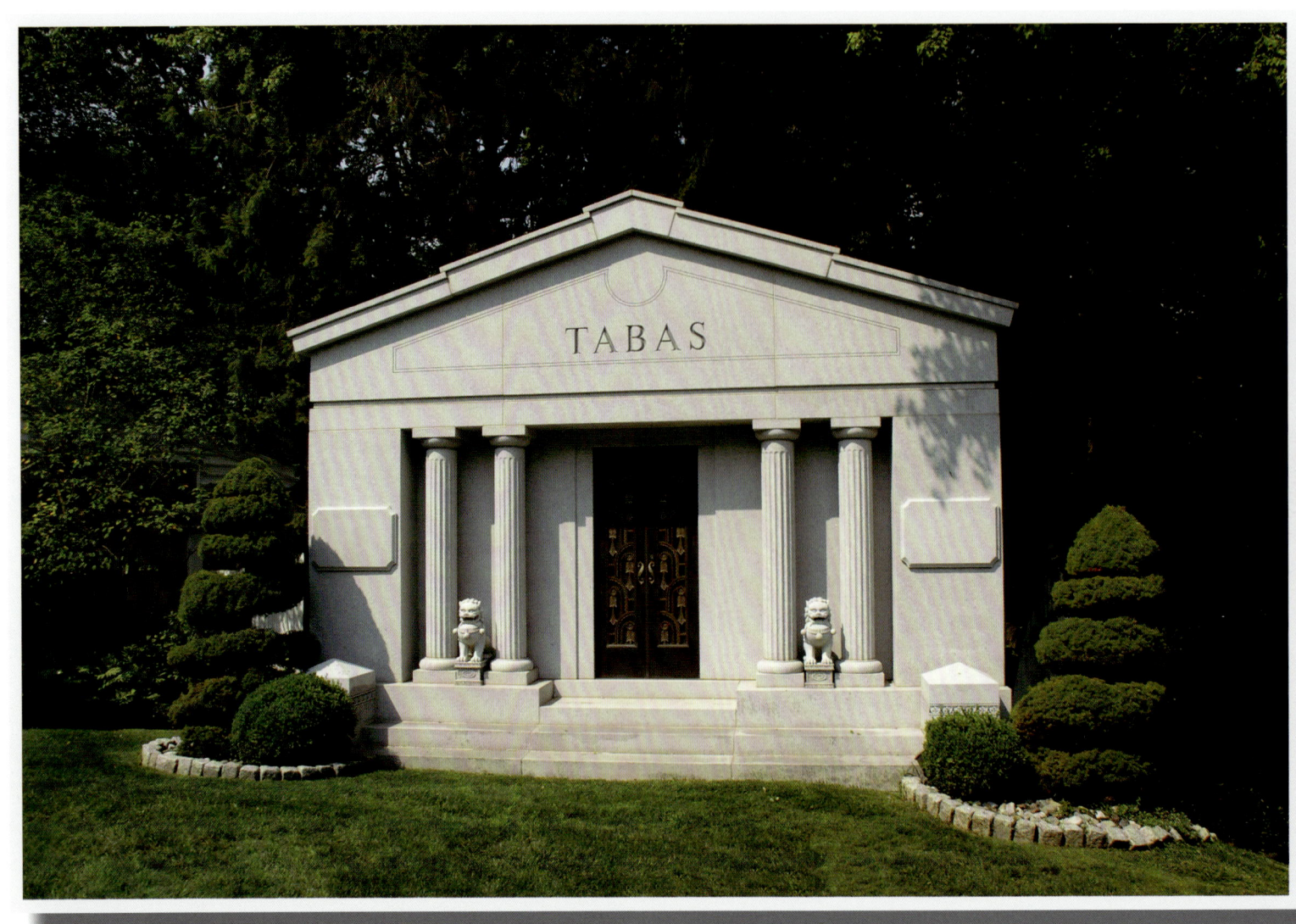

I want to stay at Acorn Farm forever. I will not be comfortable anywhere else.

Dan Tabas

Postscript

Small wonder we are a closely knit family. We have shared so much together and built our treasure chest of the past filled with experiences and memories that weave an indestructible fabric of strength, family commitment and devotion.
Evelyn Tabas

Dan, Evelyn and grandchildren pose at Acorn Farm for The Philadelphia Inquirer, 1987

In true Dan Tabas style, he found a way to spend eternity at home—he designed and had built a beautiful granite mausoleum. It looks out on the house he loved and the pasture below.

Completed in 1998, five years before Dan passed away, the four thousand square ft. mausoleum has room for "Evy," the love of his life, their children and other family members who may desire to be interred there. Acorn Farm will be held by the family in perpetuity, and the property may one day be open to the public for enjoyment and education.

DANIEL TABAS

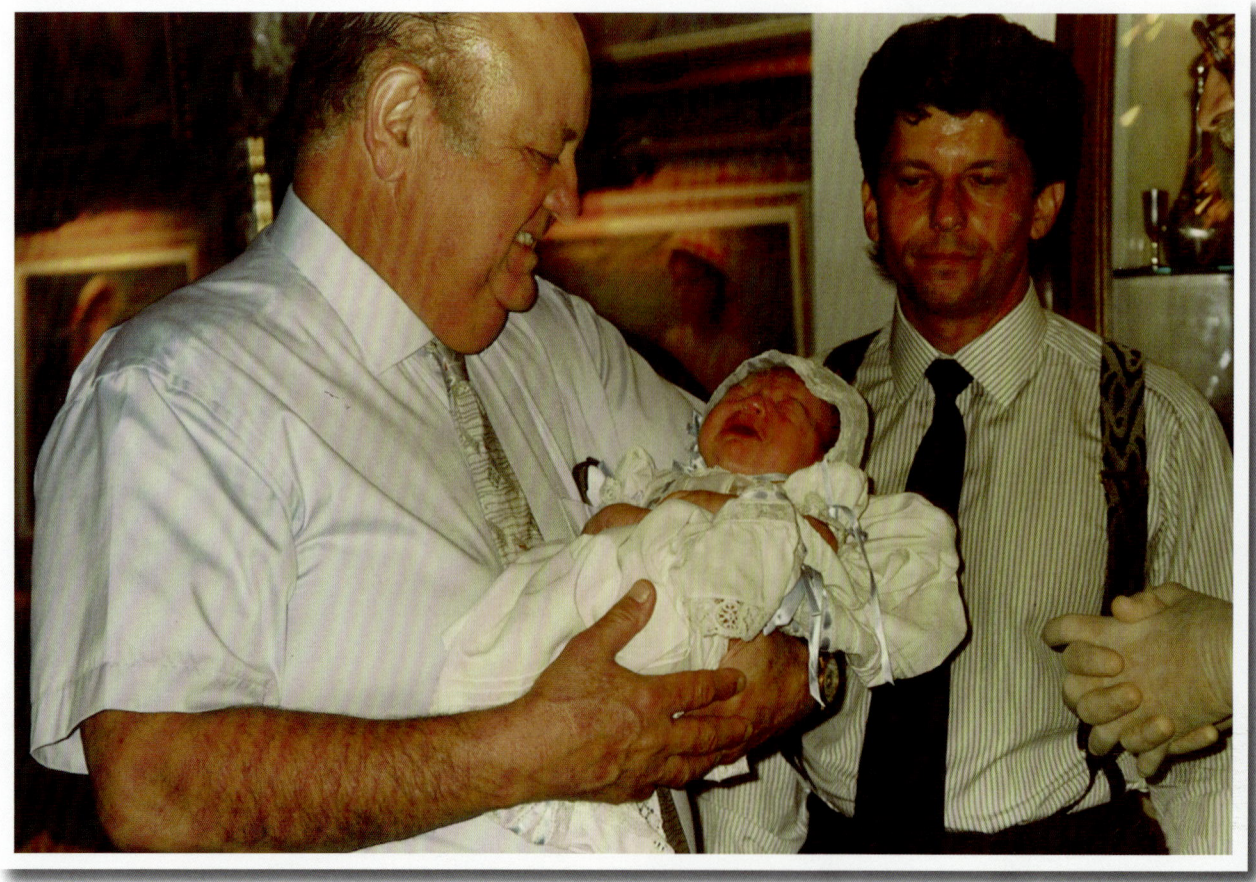

Dan cradles new grandson, Alex Stempel at his bris while father Murray Stempel III looks on, 1990

Indeed, Dan Tabas has never left those who were fortunate enough to have known him, as well as thousands more who never did, but benefited from his generosity. While he projected an image of a tough son-of-a-gun and a hard-nosed businessman, those who built a relationship with Dan knew otherwise.

The Tabas masoleum overlooks the swimming pool at Acorn Farm where Dan loved to spend time with his family (left to right) Jessica Stempel, Brittany Wurzak, Chelsea Wurzak, Major Tepper, Fitz Tepper, Susan Tabas Tepper and Zayda

Postscript

Dan and grandchildren in the front seat of Dr. Donald Rosato's four-in-hand coach at Eagle Farm for the English Speaking Union's annual charity fundraiser

"The only people who had trouble with Dan were those who tried to put something over on him," said Don Tantella Jr., whose family-owned company, Tantella and Sons Custom Cabinetry has been building cabinets, counters and display cases for the Tabas family and the various Tabas businesses since the nineteen sixties.

Jack Donnelly, CEO of L.F. Driscoll Company, Philadelphia's largest locally based construction company, was warned not to do business with Dan Tabas when Dan approached him to build the Hilton Philadelphia City Avenue. Nevertheless, Jack met with Dan and found him a "good person to do business with." Not only was Dan the first developer to pay L.F. Driscoll cash for buildings – "I'm a banker but I don't like to borrow," Dan explained – but he was the first to be involved in every aspect of construction.

Dan with daughters Linda and Jo Ann celebrate at Jessica Stempel's Bat Mitzvah

Lee and Nancy Jo Tabas commemorate Royal Bank's thirtieth anniversary with Dan and Evelyn

Over the years, Jack and Dan became good friends, and L.F. Driscoll signed-on to build Dan's last project, the Homewood Suites. Said Jack, "Other developers would tell us to just go build, and to leave them alone, but Dan was hands-on. He loved creating buildings, and he always made sure that he was getting value for his money."

Getting value for his money was always important to Dan Tabas. It explains why he scrutinized every invoice, cut out coupons and purchased grocery items on sale even if he didn't use them, why he tried to make long distance phone calls before nine in the morning or after five in the

Susan Tabas Tepper, Dan at a black tie charity event at Twelve Caesars

Postscript

afternoon when rates were lower, and why he'd drive around in a Rolls Royce looking for the best price for gasoline.

Those who knew how Dan watched his pennies, could not believe it at first when in 1980 he unveilved his new Royal Bank business card. Every card included a "sample" of the inventory of the bank, real cash! Dan always said, "If a bakery can give out a sample, why can't I?"

Dan's accumen for marketing proved that his one or two dollar bills in the fold-over business card with the trademark saying, *Who says banks don't give out samples...?*, would pay off. Those unique calling cards became one of the most successful business development strategies Dan ever used.

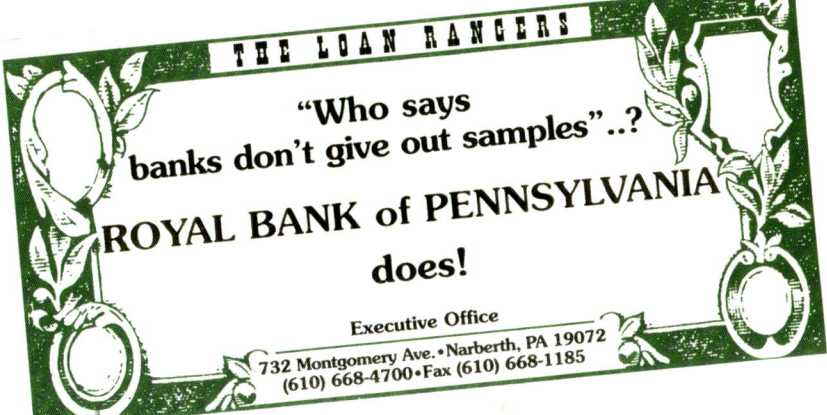

Outside cover, Dan's unique business card

Daniel M. Tabas
Chairman of the Board

Lee Evan Tabas
President & Chief Executive

Robert Royal Tabas
Senior Vice President

Murray Stempel III
Vice President

Howard Wurzak
Director

Pictured here: inside Dan's Royal Bank fold-over business card was the big conversation piece, a crisp one or two dollar bill

Fresh, crisp, clean money from

ROYAL BANK OF PENNSYLVANIA

We've lots more where this came from .. Anytime!

Susan Tabas Tepper
Director

DANIEL TABAS

Dan opening his birthday gifts

earned their everlasting loyalty.

Royal Bank America Vice-President Cindy Eastman began working with Dan in 1984. "If someone was in need," she said, Dan's generosity could not be matched."

Dan Tabas wore many hats. He was a builder. A hotelier. A banker. A confidante of political leaders. A mentor to aspiring businessman. But the hat that he was proudest of was the one he wore as patriarch of the Tabas family. He was never too busy to help a son or daughter, attend a grandchild's recital, school play, birthday party or sports game, flip burgers at a family barbecue (or his homemade latkes if it was Hanukkah), introduce a young grandchild to golf, or welcome a new family member.

Commented Jim McSwiggan: "There was a Dan Tabas who watched every nickel and dime, and there was another Dan Tabas who realized how privileged he was and had a strong desire to help people," especially the people who worked for him, which is why he

Family celebrations like this birthday party for Grandma Bluma Rome were an important part of Tabas family life

Postscript

Not long after Dan's passing and following in his footsteps, Evelyn, the six Tabas children, and their spouses formed a real estate partnership. Their goal is to follow the path to success that Dan carved out years before. Toward that end, the family partners of Poplar Realty Investments, meet regularly to build and improve communities and to grow the partnership. The siblings, spouses and Evelyn work hard to maintain the strong family bond so cherished by Dan and to continue and enhance the family business and philanthropic endeavors.

It was said of Dan Tabas that he was a "oner," a unique individual, one whose like may never be seen again. But he did leave us with a road map for success which could be summed up this way: Work hard, think big, be persistent, marry a gracious woman, teach your children the importance of family values, and always give back to your community and your nation.

Dan Tabas – the ultimate *Shtarker* – a mover and shaker, who at the end of the day got the job done.

Dan waving from the driver's seat of one of his antique cars, 1996

DANIEL TABAS

Postscript

157

DANIEL TABAS

Postscript

ACKNOWLEDGEMENTS

Zsolt Benko	Lisa Lockowitz
Betsy Z. Cohen	Jayne Oldfield
Gerry Daniel	Ivan Papurt
Fanny Davidson	Krissy Randazzo
Loree Drimak	Nicholas Randazzo
Norma Foerderer	Hon. Edward G. Rendell
Donald Gable	Merion Art and Repro
Bob Gallo	Allen L. Rothenberg
Rhona Graff	Marc Sanders
Da Vinci Graphics	Linda Tabas Stempel
Anton F. Hantig	Ben Stephan
Willie Hendley	Jonathan Tabas
Paula Hill	Robert Royal Tabas
Jacob Hope	Fitz Daniel Tabas Tepper
Apple Inc.	Kenneth L. Tepper
G-Print International	Donald J. Trump
Elaine Kolinsky	Lisa Vandiver
Heather Kustra	Diana Viglianese